Seeds in the W

Colonel Caesar
Cannonbrains of the
Black Hussars by
Anthony Powell.
'I have racked my
brains but do not
think I have
anything whatever to
put forward in the
literary line before I
was seventeen. I
really started life
being more interested
in drawing than
writing. This . . .
appeared in . . .
The Eton Candle,
when I was about
sixteen.'
2 March 1960

Seeds in the Wind

Juvenilia from W. B. Yeats to Ted Hughes

Edited with an introduction by
Neville Braybrooke

Thus, when the Sun, prepared for rest,
Hath gained the precincts of the West,
Though his departing radiance fail
To illuminate the hollow Vale,
A lingering light he fondly throws
On the dear Hills where first he rose.

from 'The Conclusion of a Poem, *Composed Upon Leaving School*' by
William Wordsworth, *aged 16*

OXFORD UNIVERSITY PRESS
1991

Oxford University Press, Walton Street, Oxford OX2 6DP

Oxford New York Toronto
Delhi Bombay Calcutta Madras Karachi
Petaling Jaya Singapore Hong Kong Tokyo
Nairobi Dar es Salaam Cape Town
Melbourne Auckland

and associated companies in
Berlin Ibadan

Oxford is a trade mark of Oxford University Press

First published in 1989 by Hutchinson
First issued as an Oxford University Press
paperback 1991

British Library Cataloguing in Publication Data
Seeds in the wind: juvenilia from W. B. Yeats to Ted Hughes.
1. English literature, 1900– . Anthologies
I. Braybrooke, Neville 1925–
820.8000912
ISBN 0-19-282840-1

Printed in Great Britain by
Clays Ltd.
Bungay, Suffolk

In Memoriam
MICHAEL ALLMAND, V.C.
1923–1944
Founder of *The Wind and the Rain*

Contents

List of Illustrations

W.B. YEATS
*Sketch of a church by W.B. Yeats while on holiday at Branscombe in Devon in the
summer of 1879*

Introduction

W. B. Yeats's first known poem, beginning 'A flower has blossomed', was written after a visit to Kilrock, when he was sixteen. It ends with these lines, which were to forecast the future pattern of his work:

Many men gathers and few may use
T[he] secret oil and the secret cruse

He sent it off to his friend Mary Cronan with this ironic note: 'My peculiaritys . . . will never be done justice to until they have become classics and are set for examinations.' How confident a young genius can be, and yet how that confidence can be shattered with the passing of time. At the memorial service held for T. S. Eliot in 1966, Ezra Pound, on coming out of Westminster Abbey, was heard to say of his own work: 'Nothing I have written is worth a thing.'

The idea for this anthology originally came to me when I was having lunch with the parson poet Andrew Young. We had been talking about the early Yeats, when I asked him if he could remember his own first poem. 'Indeed I can,' he replied. 'It was about the battle of Bannockburn and I was five years old at the time.' He then proceeded to recite it:

They fell, they fell
Till there were few to tell
How the great battle was ended.

I went home elated and feeling that his lines said almost everything that there was to be said about war.

Shortly after this, I bought a box-file and labelled it 'Twentieth Century Juvenilia'. From then onwards I began to notice how few collected works of modern authors included their earliest writings. This contrasted interestingly with the critical editions of famous authors of the past, in whose appendices there were treasures to be discovered. For instance, at the end of Milton's *Complete Poems* there was a translation of Psalm 136, which he made when a fifteen-year-old schoolboy at St. Paul's. Verse 13, about the parting of the Red Sea, ran:

The floods stood still like walls of glass
While the Hebrew bands did pass.

Then there was Wordsworth, at the age of sixteen, describing a 'horse . . . cropping audibly his later meal.' In a collection of Jane Austen's work, in the final volume, I came across the short history of England which she had completed at fifteen and in which she assured her readers that there would be very few dates. The entry about Edward V read: 'This unfortunate Prince lived so little a while that no body had time to draw his picture. He was murdered by his Uncle's Contrivance, whose name was Richard the 3rd.'

Were there, I wondered, similar treasures to be unearthed in Twentieth Century Juvenilia? For a start I had the Yeats and the Andrew Young lines on Bannockburn. I decided on an age-limit of eighteen, but on the advice of two early contributors, Robert Graves and John Cowper Powys, I lowered it to sixteen. Graves reminded me that by eighteen many of his generation were soldiers in the trenches. He also gave me two pieces of advice: 'Secure Pound, Eliot and Auden so as to make your book worthwhile (and saleable),' and 'Give no consideration to how long it will take you to do.' By way of encouragement he enclosed a batch of his own poems dating back to his Charterhouse days, in one of which, 'The Dying Knight and the Fauns', he foretells the death of his friend Raymond Rodakowski in Delville Wood, in France, in 1916.

John Cowper Powys, whom I approached next, began his reply: 'I cannot help feeling, my dear Sir, that you set the age-limit too high and that 15, or a year later, would be nearer the mark.' Then he told me how as a boy of twelve his father had taken him to Corfe Castle in Dorset, and how standing among the ruins there he had composed a poem on the spot: 'I still have it in my head, every single word of it, and I can set it down if you wish.' A week after I had accepted it he wrote back: 'I shall enjoy buying some exciting book at 87 with money earned all those years ago.'

An age limit of sixteen has obviously resulted in certain omissions. Auden and Isherwood are represented, while Spender and MacNeice are not. Arthur Miller wrote to me from America: 'I didn't begin to write until my twenties, so I'm afraid I can't send you anything.' Somerset Maugham said that he had no regard for the short stories which he had published before he was twenty-one: 'I do not wish them to be re-issued.' Anthony Burgess's youthful interests were in music. Rosamond Lehmann destroyed all her juvenile writings before she went up to Girton. David Jones, whom I visited in Harrow in the 1960s, gave this description of himself: 'I was a painter before I was a poet, and I really didn't begin to write anything until I was about twenty-seven. Up until then I was much keener on drawing.' Seamus Heaney wrote from Dublin: 'Nothing of the juvenilia sort survives before my Queen's University poem about October, composed when I was nineteen.'

There are some hundred items contained in this book – prose, poetry and miscellaneous drawings. Several of the contributors appear in surprising roles – Henry Green as a boy preacher; Malcolm Lowry as a sports correspondent; and David Gascoyne as a novelist. There are early poems by Katherine Mansfield, Ronald Firbank, Christopher Isherwood, Edward Upward, Francis King, Thomas Keneally, Alison Lurie and Piers Paul Read. George Orwell as a schoolboy of eleven adopts a flag-waving, pro-Empire stance at the outbreak of the 1914 war: a poem of his urging the young men of England to enlist is accepted by the *Henley and South Oxfordshire Standard* in October of the same year. Two domestic diaries that he kept in 1939 and 1940 completely ignore the outbreak of the Second World War – there are only entries about bird-watching, flowers and cooking recipes. Beatrix Potter shuts herself up in her bedroom in the Boltons and devises a code, so that she can keep a secret journal from thirteen onwards. An early passage from this about red deer, wooden pavement-blocks, fish-bones, mudpies and family crests has a surrealist element. In another, about the Manchester stage coach, she occasionally drops the definite article, thereby revealing her northern antecedents. In St. Louis in 1905 T. S. Eliot not only submits poems to his school magazine but also adventure stories: two of the latter, set in the South Seas, are taken by the *Smith Academy Record* and published under the initials 'T.E.' In one of them, entitled 'The Man Who was King', the natives march in procession and beat 'bhghons'. In Grove's

Musical Dictionary no such instrument is listed. The sixteen-year-old author describes them as a cross between a tin-pan and a gong. Virginia Woolf, at thirteen, writes a story making fun of feminism. Miss Smith, who has turned thirty, and given up the causes of Temperance and Women's Rights, is said to be settling into a mild 'hobly'. This is the author's first invented word and means a spinster. In 1892 Wyndham Lewis, at the age of ten, writes and illustrates an adventure story about a group of boys who land on a deserted island, which is sometimes visited by cannibals and Red Indians. They come across a castaway who turns out to be a famous English explorer and with his help build a fort to protect themselves from the onslaught of the cannibals and Indians. Some of the drawings are self-portraits of Lewis – though none of his biographers seem to have recognized this. On the last page of the story a British gunboat comes to the rescue: 'We cheered, and, we cheered and we cheered.'

Children are intrigued by repetition. It is why nursery rhymes never go out of fashion, and why children will use any opportunity to make up rhymes of their own. When I first began working on this book, a family of three boys and a girl all under ten, who lived in the cottage opposite my house, used to dance in the street round their marmalade cat singing:

Tiger Lily!
Tiger Lily!

The American poet Elizabeth Bishop, whom I met round about the same time as this, told me that the earliest rhyme that she ever composed was:

Vaseline!
Gasoline!
Vaseline!
Gasoline!

She was three at the time and the words came to her out of the air as she watched the maid polishing her shoes. Stevie Smith began to compose even earlier. Her first lines were made up when she was two:

Anna Maria amen
Pray for me and all men.

They were prompted by her seeing at church on festive occasions a large banner carried round with the words 'the gift of Anna Maria Livermore', embroidered on the silk panel. 'I learned to read pretty early,' she told me.

These rhymes and chants can be compared to seeds in the wind: some have fallen on barren soil, while others have continued to flourish. The children opposite have grown up and gone away to work in offices and shops, and probably forgotten all about their early attempts at poetry. Stevie Smith's lines about Anna Maria Livermore on the other hand carried a prophetic note, perhaps best summed up in a lecture on 'Some Impediments to Christian Commitment', which she delivered over sixty years later: 'My first steps in religious verse, I daresay, were my first in religious heresy.'

Juvenilia can be divided roughly into three categories – the entertaining, the instructive and the prophetic; but sometimes all three merge together. When the eleven-year-old Siegfried Sassoon wrote a story about a kitchen cat, with mischievous touches of autobiography included, his intention was to amuse his mother. When Jocelyn Brooke, on his eighth birthday, began writing a natural history of Surrey, his aim was to show off his knowledge of botany to his friends at school. When Virginia Woolf, at the age of eleven, saw a bird with its eyes pecked out on the steps of Talland Bay Lighthouse, her first reaction was shock, followed by an immediate desire to rush home and write about it for the family paper. Her account of this in the *Hyde Park Gate News*, dated 12 September 1892, can now be seen with hindsight as prophetic. In 1925 when she was writing *To the Lighthouse* she remarks in her diary how she regards the book as an elegy rather than a novel, and that the overriding inspiration and theme come from remembering the voices of children, the cries of sea-birds and the sound of the waves. A year later, still at work on the same book, she asks: 'What is [the book] all about?'

Her question is a perennial one among authors. Sylvia Plath at the age of fifteen begins a poem:

You ask me why I spend my life writing?

Five lines later she answers it is because:

There is a voice within me
That will not be still.

A primary source for juvenilia is school magazines and over half the contributors in this book first appeared in them. Their school-master-editors should have a place among the unsung heroes of literature. There is, though, an exception to every rule. The poet John Gray, whom I have included, was a late developer. His poem 'Writ by Me when I was Sixteen Years Old', with its phrases about 'Time's early revolutions' and 'the endless dying of a summer day', is competent but banal. Yet less than a decade later he was producing in the 1890s poetry of such distinction and quality that Oscar Wilde paid for the publication of his first volume.

Going through old copies of school magazines can be a long and tedious task. I spent several mornings at Westminster School before I came upon Angus Wilson's article on the *nouveaux pauvres* in South Kensington, whom he observed so sharply as a boy during the holidays in the late 1920s. Another find was Ted Hughes's poem on the 'Wild West', made up of over fifty couplets in one of which he rhymes 'armadillo' with 'killer'. He wrote it while at Mexborough Grammar School at the end of the Second World War.

Up until 1939 two recurring subjects in school magazines were cricket and the weather. What a surprise it must have been for the editor of the *Oxford High School Magazine*, in 1904, to find a boy writing about 'Playground Cricket', in which he argues the ball can be a stone, a piece of wood or even a potato. The boy in question was none other than T. E. Lawrence, aged sixteen. In the poetry sections of school magazines inspiration is generally thin on the ground. Yet, when it does occur, how it can lift up the spirit:

Summer! and after Summer what?
Ah! happy trees that know it not,
Would that with us it might be so.

This is Housman in the fifth form at Bromsgrove School in Worcestershire. The characteristic strain of melancholy can already be detected. E. M. Forster, who was twenty years his junior and was to become one of his most ardent admirers, during his last term at Tonbridge School in 1895 won two prizes, one for a Latin poem, one for an essay on 'The Influence of Climate and Physical Conditions upon National Character'. In the penultimate paragraph of the latter he writes:

'. . . before concluding, we must briefly touch upon the influence of change of climate and locality on a highly civilized race. We find influence is very little, sometimes hardly perceptible. An Englishman is an Englishman, whether he is on the plains of South Africa or the mountains of Upper India, and though his descendants live in these places for hundreds of years they will never in the slightest degree resemble Hottentots or Chitralis.'

Forster's authentic voice can be heard for the first time.

There are several pieces in this collection which could be classified as curiosities. Two, in the Introduction, concern James Joyce and Shaw, while in the main body of the book there is a political limerick which Pound made up when he was eleven, and the questionnaire that Graham Greene filled in at Berkhamsted School on his seventh birthday. To the question 'What are the qualities you most admire in women?' he gave the answer 'Cleanliness'. This might be said to be Greene's first interview. Nor has he ever lost his admiration for Dixon Brett, the detective hero whom he nominated then as his favourite character in fiction. In 1947 he mentioned him again in a radio talk for the BBC and refers to him twice more in his autobiography.

When James Joyce was fifteen he translated Horace's ode *O fons Bandusiae*. It made a lasting impression on him. In *Finnegans Wake* there is a reference to 'the liquick music' that the fount Bandusian plays. But Joyce's first appearance as a poet was not as a translator.

When he was nine years old he wrote a poem after Parnell's death, likening him to an eagle looking down on a rotting corpse made up of Irish politicians. So proud of it was Joyce's father that he had copies printed as a broadsheet and circulated them to friends and relations. He even went as far as having one dispatched to the Pope. Only a fragment now remains:

His quaint-perched aerie on the crags of Time
Where the rude din of this . . . century
Can trouble him no more . . .

The sting of the poem lay in its title, which was *'Et tu, Healy'*, because it was Tim Healy, one of Parnell's right-hand men, who betrayed him. But whether Joyce had Shakespeare's Brutus in mind is open to debate, for he was nothing like as precocious a reader as was Shaw, who claimed by ten to have read all the Scriptures and all Shakespeare – and, by twelve, all of Dickens, too.

My father Patrick Braybrooke, who was a cousin of Chesterton, wrote short biographies of Wells, Chesterton and Shaw; so in my youth I was naturally influenced by their writings. It was not, though, until many years later that I discovered that Shaw had written a play in his early teens entitled *Strawberrinos: or, The Haunted Winebin*. I entertained hopes of finding it in the Shaw Collection at the British Museum, but in the boxes marked 'juvenilia' there were only drawings of saints, landscapes and theatrical figures. The truth, as I learned, was that Shaw had made only one copy of his play and that this had been lost by his friend Edward McNulty, to whom he had lent it. However, McNulty did remember that the hero Strawberrinos had a series of breathless adventures, which were continually frustrated by a Mephistophelean demon. In the incantation scene the demon's song went as follows:

Fill the magic cup!
   Drink it with a will;
If it doesn't save your life
   It's pretty sure to kill –
   A saline draught and a big blue pill!

In the light of *Man and Superman* and the third act about Don Juan and the Devil, which is usually cut, the fragment has a curious relevance.

It is recorded that the first word that H. G. Wells ever wrote was 'butter'. This is a pretty word, which suggested to him happiness and plenty. Auden, at fifteen, began to write poetry simply because a friend had told him to: 'The idea previously had not entered my head.' George Orwell, when he looked back on his life, believed that the desire to disprove lies had made him into an author. Another reason for wanting to become a writer is often the need to discover one's true identity. 'Who am I?' is a recurring theme to be found in the journals and diaries of Katherine Mansfield, Virginia Woolf and W. N. P. Barbellion.

Sometimes children write poems or stories in order to re-live their dreams, flatter their friends and impress their parents (examples of all three are provided by Kathleen Raine, John Betjeman and Ronald Firbank in their works). Antonia White, when she was eight, began an essay about the copper beech, which half-way through turns into the

'Prepare ye the way . . .' Bernard Shaw's first ambition was to be a great painter, and often during his early teens he would spend hours studying the pictures in Dublin's National Gallery. St John the Baptist was drawn after a visit there, when he was fifteen.

story of how the beech leaves came to be copper-coloured. She planned it as a present for her father and down one margin pencilled the note: 'It took me nearly a month and tons of nature books to get up all this, so do not smile.' Kipling from his boarding school in Westward Ho! wrote a weekly letter to his parents in Lahore, sending them copies of all his poems; but he was not very pleased when he later learned that his father had had them privately printed under the title *Schoolboy Lyrics*. The poem 'Overheard', which gives a verbatim account of a prostitute's life, he felt could scarcely be classified as a lyric. Beryl Bainbridge's novel *Filthy Lucre* gave the thirteen-year-old author an opportunity to air her knowledge about social injustice in the London of the 1880s. The debt to Dickens and Robert Louis Stevenson is noticeable – and acknowledged. Eliot's earliest surviving lyric, modelled on Ben Jonson, begins:

If Time and Space, as Sages say,
  Are things which cannot be,
The sun which does not feel decay
  No greater is than we . . .

Tracking down sources, especially in Eliot, has become an academic pastime. Reading patterns in early youth are frequently influenced by the unexpected, such as Graham Greene's addiction at the age of six to the adventures of Dixon Brett. Literary taste too is often formed on no higher criterion than 'I know what I like.' There is also the reverse of the coin – 'I know what I don't like.' Beatrice Webb, who chronologically has first place in this collection, came to the conclusion in her mid-teens that *Jane Eyre* was 'an impure book'; she thought that Charlotte Brontë's presentation of love was of 'a feverish, almost lustful passion'. She may have been envious. Even from the first entry in her diary, dated 1868 when she was ten, there can be no doubt about the high moral and rather priggish attitude which she adopted towards fiction, and her fear that a continual diet of it could destroy 'a young mind'.

Throughout this anthology I have left unchanged the various authors' use of capital letters and punctuation. In places where it is obvious that words have been left out I have restored them in square brackets; occasionally, too, I have added notes and footnotes to clarify the texts. Spelling has presented a problem, because so perfect has it been in some cases I suspect a parent or schoolmaster-editor might have had a hand. There are, though, some nice phonetic spellings – 'Mrs Kreston . . . langwidly sat down & calved a chicken.' That is Firbank in his unfinished novel *Lila*, begun when he was just ten.

At the end of the book I give the sources from which I have drawn my material, although three-quarters of it has never been published before in a general sense. School magazines have limited circulations and are not for public sale. In 1912 *The Pistol Troop Magazine*, edited by the nine-year-old Evelyn A. St.J. Waugh from his home, had a circulation of two – the typed copy and the carbon one: there were contributions by his father and his brother Alec and an illustrated short story by himself about hidden treasure entitled *'Multa Pecunia'*. Katherine Mansfield's three poems, written when she was fourteen, were transcribed earlier this year from one of her New Zealand notebooks by Margaret Scott, the editor of her Letters. When Dylan Thomas was attending Swansea Grammar School his friend and contemporary, the future composer Daniel Jones set several of his poems to music: Jones' score for the poem, beginning 'Hourly I sigh', has never previously been printed.

Looking through the contents page of this collection one suddenly becomes conscious of the ups and downs of literary fashion. 'The longer your book takes you, the more you will see this,' Robert Graves said to me in 1959. In the late 1940s and early 1950s Jocelyn Brooke's work was receiving solo reviews in all the serious papers. But in the final ten years of his life until his death in 1966, he slipped into the grey world of forgotten authors and was unable to find a publisher for any of his works. Now it is a different story: they are all in paperback and a full-length biography has been commissioned. Ruth Pitter, who is in her nineties, is not listed in the *Oxford Companion to English Literature*. Yet she was the first woman poet to receive the Queen's Gold Medal for Poetry, and Philip Larkin, one of her staunchest admirers, gave more space to her work in his *Oxford Book of Twentieth Century Verse* than he did to the work of William Plomer, John Heath-Stubbs or Lawrence Durrell. In the mid-1940s when I was editing the little review *The Wind and the Rain* I used sometimes to receive poems with covering letters signed 'From Starving & Forgotten John Betjeman'. Roy Campbell on the other hand, who was then my near neighbour in Kensington Church Street, preferred to be paid for his poems in pints at the Catherine Wheel.

Juvenilia has frequently survived on the flimsiest scraps of paper.

Wyndham Lewis's story 'Good Times', which is now carefully preserved at Cornell, was in a very tattered state when it was acquired by the university after his death in 1957. Editing this book I have often thought of the faithful literary pilgrims in the last century who would travel up to visit the home of an elderly lady in Scotland, and there be shown the boyish scrawl of her son's first attempts to translate Virgil. On the folder containing these fragile sheets were written the words: 'My Walter's first lines', followed by the date 1782. The author of the Waverley novels was ten years old. His versions of Virgil, and a little later of Horace, won his schoolmaster's applause.

A noticeable difference between the juvenilia of past centuries, and that of the Twentieth, is the absence of classical translations. In this anthology only James Joyce tries his hand at Horace. There is also a noticeable lack of classical allusions: H. G. Wells and Conrad Aiken mention Homer and Xerxes, but only in passing.

The novel *The Desert Daisy* by H. G. Wells, which is the longest item in the book, was found among his papers after his death in 1946. He wrote it between his twelfth and thirteenth birthday, when he was living in Bromley, and much of it was planned as he wandered about the streets and nearby countryside, visualizing himself as a great emperor, ordering cannons to be brought up from Croydon so that a successful attack might be launched against the enemy at Keston Fish Ponds. 'The only vivid and inspiring things that history fed me with,' he was to say later, 'were campaigns and conquests.'

In Chapter IV of the novel the narrator, realizing how difficult it is to immortalise a hero, expresses the wish: 'Ah! that I was Homer!' But when the eighth chapter was reached, and the book completed, all modesty deserted the young Wells. On the cover he put his own rave reviews – half seriously, half mockingly. 'Beats *Paradise Lost* into eternal smash' went one attributed to the *Naily News*. Another went: 'Descriptions of the Battles sublime!' This he attributed to *The Telephone*, although the telephone itself had only come into commercial use during the late 1870s when he was writing the novel. Then as always, Wells had an eye on the shape of things to come.

August 1989

W. B. Yeats 1865–1939

A Flower has Blossomed . . .

aged 16

A flower has blossomed, the world heart core
The petels and leves were a mo[o]n white flame colour
A gathred the flower, the ‹soul› colourless love
The aboundant meadow of fate and fame
Many men gathers and few may use
T[he] sacret oil and the sacret cruse

Beatrice Webb 1858–1943

Castles in the Air

aged 10

I am quite confident that the education of girls is very much neglected in the way of their private reading. Take, for instance, a girl of nine or ten years old, she is either forbidden to read any but child's books, or she is let loose on a good library; Sir Walter Scott's novels recommended to her as charming and interesting stories – 'books that cannot do any possible harm', her adviser declares. But the object in reading is to gain knowledge. A novel now and then is a wise recreation to be offered to a growing mind; it cultivates the imagination, but taken as the continual nourishment, it destroys many a young mind. The whole of their thought (for a child of nine or ten spends little or no thought on her lessons) is wasted on making up love scenes, or building castles in the air, where she is always the charming heroine without a fault. I have found it a serious stumbling-block to myself; whenever I get alone I always find myself building castles in the air of some kind; it is a habit that is so thoroughly immured in me that I cannot make a good resolution without making a castle in [the] air about it.

Mormons

aged 15

Salt Lake City is not to be compared with any town in England or America; it is so utterly different from anything I have ever seen. The streets are very wide, and on both sides of them flow beautiful streams of crystal water brought from the mountains ten to twenty miles off.

It is through this water that Brigham Young and his few followers transformed this sandy desert into a fertile farm. The houses are for the most part low, built rather in the French style, and of wood whitewashed over, with green shutters and doors. This gives the city a fresh innocent appearance, especially as . . . each house has its garden and orchard.

The Tabernacle is by far the most important building in Salt Lake City; then come Brigham's two houses, 'The Lion' and 'The Beehive', and a very pretty villa he is building for Mrs Amelia Young, his last and most beloved wife. Most of his other wives either live in one of his two houses, or else have small houses round them in his garden. The only one of his wives we saw was Mrs Eliza Young, No 17, who separated from him, and is now lecturing on Mormonism all over America. She was staying at Walker's Hotel; she was rather a pretty woman at a distance, but decidedly coarse when you examined her near.

In the afternoon we went to hear Anson Pratt, an Apostle, and one of the original founders of the Mormon creed. During the summer the service is held in the Tabernacle, but as it is built of wood they are afraid of heating it, which of course makes it impossible to use in the winter. So each ward has its own meeting-house where they assemble on Sundays during the winter months. We went to the 13th ward. The congregation was mostly of the working men's class. They seemed to be very attentive and earnest in their devotions. I noticed here particularly the dejected look of the women, as if they had continually on their mind their inferiority to their lords and masters. The service was begun by a hymn. Then a decidedly clever looking man (a bishop) stood up and recited a prayer, in itself very good, but said more in a tone of 'we only demand what we have a right to' than of humble supplication. Then the sacrament was handed round and another hymn sung, after which Anson Pratt got up and began his discourse.

The first passage is thought to be the earliest surviving passage of Beatrice Webb's diary, and is undated. The second is dated 1 November 1873, and with it her diary can be said to begin in earnest. 'It was her father's custom, whenever he went to inspect his railway interests in Canada and the United States, to take some of the family with him,' write Norman and Jeanne MacKenzie in their editorial notes to Volume 1 of *The Diary of Beatrice Webb: 1873–1892* (1982).

A. E. Housman 1859–1936

Summer

aged 15

Summer! and over brooding lands
The noonday haze of heat expands.
A gentle breeze along the meadows
Lifts a few leaflets on the trees;
But cannot stir the clouds that lie
Motionless on the dreaming sky,
And cannot stir the sleeping shadows
As motionless upon the leas.
Summer! and after Summer what?
Ah! happy trees that know it not,
Would that with us it might be so.
And yet, the broad-flung beechtree heaves
Through all its slanting layers of leaves
With something like a sigh. Ah no!
'Tis but the wind that with its breath
To them so softly murmureth;
For them hath still new sweets in store
And sings new music evermore;
Only to us its tones seem sighs,
Only to us it prophesies
Of coming Autumn, coming Death.

Letter Home

aged 16

My dear Mama,
                    I cannot say
That much, since you have gone away,
Has happened to us, so of course
I must fall back on that resource, –
That great resource, which o'er this earth
Precedence holds, and which is worth
All other topics put together,
I mean, (I need not say) THE WEATHER.
The weather has been clear and bright,
The sun has shed a vivid light
So hot and torrid, that my stout
Aunt Mary has not ventured out,
Until the shades of evening fall
And gentle moonbeams silver all,
When lunatics are wont to prowl
As also are the bat and owl.
Then to the shadowy garden fly
My relative and Clem and I.
Clemence becomes a fancied knight
In visionary armour dight
And waves her lance extremely well,
Terrific but invisible.
I turn into a dragon dire
Breathing imaginary fire,
Obscuring all the starry sky
With vapours seen by fancy's eye.
Aunt Mary is a hapless maid
Imprisoned in a dungeon's shade
And spreading streams of golden hair
Impalably upon the air.
Such is she 'neath the moon's pale ray,
But during all the burning day
At open window she had heard

The notes of many a chattering bird,
Receiving quite an education
From all this feathered conversation.
'Look here! Look here!' one of them cries,
'Peter' another one replies,
(Perhaps a Roman Catholic bird)
And scarcely has he said this word
When one of a more ferocious mind
Screams out in fury 'Whip behind!'
And scarcely has his clamour ceased
When shrieks arise of 'You're a beast!'
Another, rest one moment brings,
Saying in French, pacific things,
Then one (piano) 'pretty Dick!'
One more (crescendo) 'Quick! Quick! Quick!
(Forte) Look here! Look here!' once more
And so da capo, as before.

For other sound thine ears delight,
For other shapes are in thy sight,
Where the pellucid Thames flows by
The Tower of English liberty,
Where he of Stoke[1] brings forth his din
(That famous ass in lion's skin),
Waves his umbrella high in vain
And shakes off dewdrops from his mane.
Or where, high rising over all,
Stands in the Cathedral of St. Paul
And in its shadow you can span
Our late lamented ruler, Anne:
Or where the clouds of legend lower
Around the medieval Tower,
And ghosts of every shape and size
With throttled throats and staring eyes
Come walking from their earthy beds
With pillow-cases on their heads.

[1]Edward Vaughan Kenealy, who had been elected MP for Stoke-on-Trent two months before this letter.

And various ornaments beside
Denoting why or how they died
Or where all beasts that ever grew
All birds, all fish, all reptiles too
Are congregated at the Zoo.
Where singing turtles soothe the shade
And mackerel gambol through the glade,
Where prisoned oysters fain would try
Their wonted flight into the sky,
And the fierce lobster in its rage
Beats its broad wings against its cage,
Or where soft music's rise and fall
Re-echoes through St. James' Hall,
Or where of painting many a one
Adorn the House of Burlington,
Or where the gilded chariots ride
Resplendent through the Park of Hyde.
Or where, when he's been doomed to feel
Death from Laertes' poisoned steel,
The lifeless corpse of Hamlet draws
Resuscitation from applause;
Or where –
                You will perceive perhaps
Those 'where's' have come to a collapse;
'The waxen wings that flew so high'
Etcetera
        Mama, goodbye.

You will be glad to hear it told
Father has lost almost his cold,
Miss Hudd is *healthy*, and all we
Are well as we could wish to be.
Our love for you we all declare
And our relations at Kildare,[1]
Hopes for your pleasure in London,
And I remain your loving son.
                                AEH

[1]House belonging to Lucy Housman's family.

Rudyard Kipling 1865–1936

The Carolina

aged 10

Aūrŏrā rose in a cloudless sky
And looked on all so beamingly
Portsmouth's dark walls stood out so bright
Amid the flood of beaming light
A vessel from the harbour came
The Carolina was her name
With Stun'sails set and royals too
Over the billows she lightly flew
Three hundred souls bouds[1] for London town
Each one doomed Alas! to drown
For o'er the deck Death's dark shape hung
Loud and weird were the songs he sung
The sun had set there came clouds and rain
The ship was never seen again
She had sunk on a rock and then gone down
With 300 souls bound for London town
She had sunk like lead with no canvas rent
And never a spar or catline bent
The waves sighed mid the masts of the wreck
And fishes darted athwart the deck
Down, down, she lies full 50 fathom down
Does the Carolina bound for London town.

[1]bouds=bound.

Overheard

aged 16

So the day dragged through,
And the afternoon brought the spangles,
   The sawdust smell, the tights,
   The flickering, flashing lights,
      The smile to acknowledge the cheer
As the rider skips and jangles
   The bells. Ye gods! – 'twas queer
How the young equestriennes flew.

A programme relished, I lay
   Back in my seat to gaze
On the faces around, to hear what folk say,
While the orchestra rattled and roared,
   Murdering popular lays –
It was hot, too, and I felt bored.

Then a voice from behind, a rustling of dress,
   The step of a man, a silence to settle,
A babble of children (how they push,
The little ones, making your coat a mess),
A silence to settle, and after a gush
   Of small talk, I sat and waited,
   Shutting my eyes till the stream abated.
'Twas a tale of trouble, told in a rush.

Who was the speaker? I turned to see –
   A sharp little saucy face,
No whit abashed, gazing at me
With bead-eyes, curiously,
   With a petulant child's grimace,
As I shifted, moving her feet
   From the chair where they'd taken root,
   For the time at least; then again
I listened. Fast and fleet

She poured out the queer little words to her friend –
(A sort of an overgrown brute).
I heard it out to the end –
   A story of pain.
   Here you have it, in fine
     (Her words, not mine):
   'Tried for luck in London –
                Voilà tout!
   Failed, lost money, undone;
   Took to the streets for a life.
              Entre nous,
   It's terrible uphill strife,
   Like all professions – too filled.
   And now I'm in lodgings hard by,
   Au quatrième, up in the sky.
   Visit me by and by,
They're furnished, but oh – so cold,
   So cold!'

There the queer little voice was stilled;
   She moved to a further chair
   And left me sitting there
     To think on the story told –
   Not to me, but to her friend –
Of a life that had only one end,
   And for burden, 'Oh, so cold!'

Have you ever seen on the face
   Of a child a sort of despair,
   A comical hopeless air,
When a toy won't work, or a doll won't cry,
Or a cart runs awkwardly?
   Well, I saw it there
   As she moved to a further chair.
She'd broken some toy she had –
Or, was it a life gone bad?

Roses

aged 16

Roses by babies' rosier fingers pressed
In wondering amazement. Later, youth
Attired in knickerbockers, flings them by
Contemptuously. Lovers' offerings then,
Much kissed and withered. Staid and sober age
In snug, suburban villas rears them last:
The world at large is dowered with their thorns!

'The Carolina' is probably one of Kipling's earliest surviving poems and was signed
J. R. Kipling. Andrew Rutherford, in his edition of *Early Verse by Rudyard Kipling
1879–1889* (1986), points out that in marking Aūrŏrā thus, the poet 'has made two
false quantities out of three. Clearly he had not been introduced to Latin at this stage.'
One version of 'Overheard' has eight extra lines at the end, the last of which is: 'She
has my prayers if they're any avail.' 'Roses' was prompted by Jaques' speech 'All the
world's a stage' in *As You Like It*.

H. G. Wells 1866–1946

The Desert Daisy

aged 12–13

CHAPTER I

The King of Clubs was in his Council Chamber.

There was with him. The Prince Bishop of Deuceace & the Commander in Chief of the Army & Navy.

They were playing at 'Push Pin'.

(To those who are ignorant I will explain that the Game of Push Pin is a very simple game suitable for ordinary children, Idiots or Kings.)

The King was striving to win with all his might (& that was'ent much), perspiration streamed down his face. He was losing rapidly both temper & cash.

Suddenly an attendant entered & said; 'Sire, Two 'Eralds from the King of Spades desires to read an a-nouncement to you.'

Using a very bad word indeed (I am sorry to say), the King seated himself on a throne hard by. The Commander in Chief (a type of physical power) placed himself on the right of the throne; The Prince Bishop (moral power) put himself on the left.

The Heralds then entered. After blowing his trumpet, the first Herald commenced:

'Whereas & not withstanding: Whereby & therefore! You Egroggetippe King of the once renowned & pussiant, now feeble & helpless Clubs!, You Egroggetippe (not unjustly called the ace or ass of Clubs), Lord of the Minced Pie (one and indivisible).' (At this point the King was seen to hand his sceptre to the Prince Bishop. He then gradually removed his crown & royal robes handing them to the same person). Meanwhile the Herald:

'You did send men or a man in the darkness of night into the Laundrey of our Sovereign Lord Methusala the Great! King of Spades & Governor General of the World, with intent to do grievous harm unto our Sovereign Lord aforesaid by ripping up the stitches of our

Sovereign Lord's best britches or breeches (as some hath it) when hung out to dry, thereby causing our said Sovereign Lord to imperil the future welfare of his soul by wearing his Everyday Britches (or Breeches as some hath it) on the Lord's day. We do demand herewith payment of the sum of twopence halfpenny being the sum charged for renewing the stitches in the said Britches (or Breeches as some hath it) or we do declare immediately War against thee & th—'

The Herald never finished the sentence for the King (who as I remarked before, had been gradually removing his various incumberances) suddenly sprang at him with the fierceness of a tiger.

The other Herald soon joined in the combat & the Commander in Chief followed his Example. All was confusion for nearly an hour.

Meanwhile where was the Bishop? Alas! The crown, sceptre and robes had been too much for his honesty.

Wrapping them up in his robe he had fled & was already a good mile away from the Kingdom of Clubs, in the Kingdom of Spades.

★ ★ ★

The Combat raged fiercely for more than an hour in the Castle. The Combatants were then separated & the King asked for his crown.

The Prince Bishop was not to be seen.

They searched high & low . . . But they did not find either Prince Bishop or crown.

What *was* to be done?

CHAPTER II

Directly it was known that the Clubs were to fight the Spades, a Council was held at which it was decided to: 'Prosecute the war with vigour to the honor safty & welfare of our Sovereign Lords' dominions' & also to: 'Leave the sole command & direction of the war unto our faithful servant Edieotte "Commander in Chief of the Army & Navy of Clubs".'

Both of which were carried unanimous.

The next day the Commander in Chief got up early & repaired with his Drummer (who was the only soldier then in the army except the Commander) to a dust heap outside the Castle Gate.

Here they raised the national flag & sang the national anthem.

The Drummer then commenced playing national tunes & the Commander stood in a tremendous attitude with a pocket book ready to enrol recruits.

He had not long to wait.

The populance absolutly flocked to his standard & 'ere one-o-clock he had three men & a boy & a humpback in a line behind him.

He then repaired to a neighbouring cook shop & had a sausage & some porter.

When he returned he found that the humpback had deserted, but not at all discouraged he set to work & soon enlisted a butcher boy & a beggar with only one arm & leg.

He then marched his army into barracks & went back to the palace to take a quiet tea with the King.

He found the King gradually recovering from his grief at the loss of his crown & vowing vengance against the King of Spades whom he considered as the prime cause of his losses.

He listened eagerly to the plans of Edieotte & they spent three hours discussing the plan of the campaign & in looking over maps &c. & talking of maps I may as well give the reader a map; so that when I come to giving a full account of the campaign, he will be able to follow me without my wasting my time in description.

The map I give is a facsimle of one belonging to the Commander and is supposed to be the most truthful one in existance.

Next morning the army was called out & divided thus.

Infantry of the line: two men.
Skirmishers (irregular): that boy.
Cavalry: The Butcher Boy.
Artillery: The Beggar.

It was decided also that the Cavalry should go on foot under the name of the 'Dismounted Cavalry' because Horses happened to be scarce at the time, & that the Artillery should not be allowed guns because guns were *so* expensive.

Uniforms were then distributed & the army was informed that it was to march that afternoon.

As soon as the news was known, the friends, parents, relations & guardians of the Troops came flocking to the barracks to say goodbye, & as the soldiers of the army had on an average each more than twenty relations the ceremony was very touching.

In fact 'that boy' had a very narrow escape from death by smothering in the affectionate embrace of a fond aunt of advanced age.

He was *black in the face* when rescued.

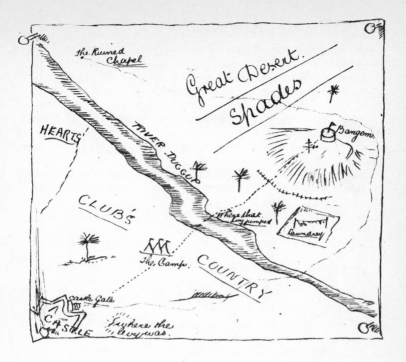

At last however the army dragged itself away & at about three in the afternoon commenced its march. By night they reached the Duggup & camped (see map).

And next morning early the[y] prepared to cross the Duggup.

CHAPTER III

Early next morning the army marched out & prepared to cross the Duggup.

General Edieotte marched his army up until they were in a line with the bank.

He then discovered that there were no boats.

Giving his army orders not to move he proceeded down the river bank in search of boats.

He was unsuccessful and after pacing about for an hour or two he returned.

What was his surprise when he returned to behold nothing.

His army had disappeared!

Controlling a violent impulse to bolt, he proceeded to the place where he had left them, to find a clue by close investigation.

Around lay all the marks of a violent struggle.

The grass was trodden down in many places.

Hoof-marks were deeply indented in the soft ground. Suddenly his eye caught something in the grass.

At first he thought it a piece of some unfortunate, chopped to bits. Nearer investigation proved it to be a pork chop.

Suddenly before him rose a figure out of the ground.

At first he thought it an ambush but nearer & clearer views shewed it to be 'that boy again.'

'Oh Gineral'; he cried as soon as he saw who it was: 'Oh Gineral wee've bin & gone & done it now.'

'What?' said the General; 'What have you been doing with the army? Where is it? Eigh'?

'Oh Gineral'; sobbed the youth, his emotion overcoming him; 'Oh Gineral. They bin & gone & run it.'

'Go on my boy'; said the General, deadly calm; 'Go on.'

'Yus sir'; said that boy; 'Soon after you was gone, Rigment number one infntry purposed as we should just jump the Duggup for a little divarshon until you came back.'

'Right sey I, an' in another minute or so all the blessed boys were on the tother side of the duggup 'cept the artillery & he hade'nt no legs to jump.'

'So when we got on tother side sey Rigment number two infantry: "Wont it be jolly fun just to storm Bangem fort afore the Gineral comes back".

'Glorious we all sey & up the slopes we went at double quick.'

'Their Garrison being all asleep at the time we hadent no difficulty in gettin' rid of em for we tied em up afore they was awake & took em down the slopes & settled their hashes at double quick.

'Well we was just getting things straight for you when you came back when suddenly cavalry cries out: "Jack 'eres a bull a 'eading straight for us."

'Well directly we heard that, we all started private retrograde movements in all directions.'

'I remember rolling down the slope somehow & gettin' 'cross the river somehow & the next thing as I remember is gettin' up & seein' you with a pork chop in your hand staring about sort of dazed like as tho' you was somewhat surprised at ——'

A trampling of hoofs, a bellow, a sharp stinging sensation behind & the Commander in chief of the Army of Clubs was in the air. He caught one glimpse of the earth, which appeared flying rapidly away from him. There was a blow on the back and all was oblivion.

★ ★ ★

Late that day a straggler wearing the uniform of the Grand Army arrived at the Castle & told his tale of disaster.

Soon another arrived confirming the news.

Then another.

The General returned not.

Neither did the skirmishers.

All was dismay.

The King took the command & had the fortification of the castle repaired.

Suddenly a ray of hope dawned on the afflicted Clubs.

The King's Great Grand Aunt (who had apartments in the castle) was heard to say: 'as shee'd bin' tould when a child as 'When the Crown goes the Clubs go.' When this was told the King he issued notices that if anyone would regain the Crown he would give him or her half his domains & the hand of the Princess Amelia (if he chose to take it).

Now the Princess Amelia was a simple maiden of 39! . . .

Clubs waited for a deliverer

CHAPTER IV

Clubs continued to wait for a deliverer.

At last he came.

Lionel Geffory de Thompson Smythe was a youth of noble blood and uncommon tall aspirations.

The enterprise just suited his noble spirit; he accepted the King's offer & announced to all the world that he would start immediately.

He started.

★ ★ ★

Meanwhile concerning the Prince Bishop.

If the reader will refer to the map, he will see proceeding from the castle gate in the left-hand corner, two lines – one dotted & one plain. Now if the reader will follow the plain line he will find that it follows a winding course until it reaches a ruined chapel in the centre of the Great Desert.

This was the uneventful course of the Prince Bishop.

Here he started business as a hermit until such time as the loss of the crown should be forgotten.

Then he would repair to some respectable pawnbroker & settle the matter.

★　★　★

The adventure had started.

Everything seemed to aid him.

The Prince Bishop had started in the rainy season, or rather I should say at the end of the rainy season.

The continual dry season that had followed had baked & parched the ground, leaving his tracks as clear as though they had been cast in iron.

This greatly aided de Smythe.

The Prince Bishop had worn hobnail boots with one particular nail wanting.

By these means de Smythe was able to track him to the banks of the Duggup with ease.

De Smythe was then brought to a standstill.

Should he plunge forward into the Spade country or return & report progress to the King.

He determined to plunge.

He plunged.

In a minute he was on the ground of the King of Spades on the trail.

Suddenly he heard a hoarse bellow that chilled his very blood.

It was that bull again.

Two alternatives were before him.

Fight or Bolt.

He determined to fight.

He fought.

It is perfectly useless to describe the fight; the artist may perhaps be more sucessful in drawing it.

Ah! that I was Homer!

If I was, de Smythe would not have long to wait for someone to immortalize him.

As it is he has three pictures devoted to the subject.

One picture is allygorical & represents: In the centre; de Smythe in triumph. To the right; 'The Present' viewing the scene with astonishment from the fastness of a Fir Tree. To the left; Posterity looking back amazed. There are also a few dozen angels & heathen goddesses scattered about, not to mention a distant view of the Great Desert & a few other trifles which we leave to the reader to discover.

★ ★ ★

Having cut the bull into fragments de Smythe chose a few tit bits & departed in triumph leaving the carcass to the wolves & jackasses.

Pushing forward rapidly de Smythe skirted 'Bangem' & at last as the sun was setting found himself on the bounds of the boundless desert.

'Ah' he said; 'Tomorrow will be my last day on the trail' & he smiled grimly. He then stretched his manly form on the sand & was soon sleeping as sound as a babe.

He was awakened by a smothering sensation.

Opening his eyes he saw with terror & grief that he was embedded firmly in the sand! A sandstorm had risen in the night & covered him!

Twas useless to struggle.

Starvation stared him in the face.

He was in despair.

Suddenly he saw a black speck on the horizon.

At first he thought it was the Prince Bishop but as it came nearer he saw that it was a lovly maiden.

As soon as she saw him she cried; 'Hullo ole' chap wait a nour & Ill come & dig you out in the twinkling of a bedpost.'

She passed on.

He waited an hour & she came out.

He waited another & then she appeared with a shovel & commenced digging round his roots rapidly. In ten minutes she had rooted him up & he was free.

No sooner was he extracted than dropping on his knees before her he exclaimed; 'Oh my deliverer. Make me a happy or a miserable man for ever. Will you be my wife?'

'I guess I will'; she replied. 'There's a ruined chapel over thar where a hermit lives so you can tie the knot at once.

'My neam's the Desert Daisy'; she added; 'if your a goin' to have banns put up.'

'Ah!' cried de Smythe impetuously; 'Guide me to this hermit; 'tis the man I want.'

'All right;' said the DD; 'follow me.'

In three minutes they were outside the ruined chapel.

Giving the DD orders to guard the door & to let no one escape, de Smythe took a short run & leapt lightly in through the window.

The Hermit was making a late breakfast of Ostritch eggs. Directly he saw who it was he fell on his knees with a loud yell of; 'Mercy'

'You shall have it' said de Smythe; 'if you will marry me to the young 'ooman outside & go half shares in the crown.'

'Anything'; sobbed the Bishop; still on his knees; 'Anything for a quiet life.'

★ ★ ★

That day the ceremony was celebrated.

★ ★ ★

That night at half-past twelve the bishop rose cautiously. He listened for a moment to see if both his companions were asleep. A duet of snores reassured him. Stepping cautiously he made his way to a neglected corner of the edifice.

He stopped to listen for a moment then putting his arm into a large hole, pulled forth the crown & sceptre & wrapped them in his robe.

Three minutes more & he was fleeing rapidly away from the Hermitage. Suddenly he stopped for a moment & turning round he made a defiant sign at the venerable ruin.

He then turned & continued his course.

<h3 style="text-align:center">CHAPTER VI</h3>

As soon as it was known that a bull was loose somewhere near the seat of war both sides fell back into their respective castles & put their fortifications in repair.

At last the King of Spades (who was very badly provisioned) was forced to send a man out to investigate.

The man advanced some little way without seeing anything. He then came on a leg of mutton. Farther on there was a sirloin of beef. There was also a veal & ham pie & lots of gravy scattered about. All these articles were cooked in a manner that made the finders mouth water.

He, at first, was unable to think how they came there, but after a long reflection the idea occurred to him; 'Someone's kilt the bool & the Sun's bin & cooked him.'

He then returned to the castle in triumph.

Directly it was known in the castle of the King of Spades that the bull was killed, the army was called out, reviewed & ordered to prepare for marching on the morrow.

Early in the morning of the next day they started.

By 10 o-clock they reached the Duggup, which they jumped & by one they were in front of the Club's Castle.

King Groggenose had been watching their advance & as soon as they paused, he sallied forth at the head of all his available troops, the

45

Princess Amelia bringing up the rear with a frying-pan.

The Spades would soon have been defeated had not the King of Spades just then arrived on the field accompanied by his head cook & another.

This turned the tide & the Clubs fled Helterskelter in all directions. King Groggenose led the retreat & arrived safe that night in the Kingdom of Hearts &, not losing any time, the next morning he opened business as a pawnbroker, distinguishing his shop by hanging out a sign with an inverted club on it to show that things were upside down with him.

He however prospered in business & had his sign gilded to show things were brightening up.

Hence the three gilded balls of a Pawnbroker.

Meanwhile the King of Spades had torn the Club banner down & raised his own & began to imagine that he was the most powerful monarch on Earth.

★ ★ ★

When de Smythe awoke & found that the Prince Bishop had betrayed him he used a great many bad words & vowed he would follow him to the End of the Earth & slay him.

So he started.

CHAPTER VII

The Ex-King of Clubs was in his shop.

Nothing unusual had occurred to mark that day.

There had been no Comets in the sky.

No dire Earthquakes.

Nothing.

But that day was to be the turning-point of his fortunes.

Suddenly a customer entered.

He looked round for the proprietor.

His eye lighted on the King & he started back amazed.

The King was equally amazed for there in front of him stood the Prince Bishop of Deuceace!!!

Directly the Bishop recovered from his surprise he turned to flee, but the King was too quick for him.

The fight with the Heralds was nothing to it.

The Prince Bishop was thrown down & nearly throttled in a few minutes.

Just at this crisis a third party entered the shop.

It was de Smythe.

Seeing the state of affairs, & the crown & sceptre rolling about on the floor, he soon formed his plans.

Picking the crown and sceptre up he decamped leaving the Combatants still warmly engaged.

It did not take long for the King to throttle the Prince Bishop &, as soon as he had done so, he turned round for the crown & sceptre.

In a moment he saw they were gone & rightly guessing the cause he rushed to the door, just in time to see de Smythe disappear round the corner.

In a moment he was after him.

For the first ten minutes they ran rapidly.

They then settled down into a rapid trot.

The King soon began to gain slowly on de Smythe.

On they ran until they were out of Hearts & in Clubs.

Suddenly de Smythe doubled & headed straight for the Duggup, which he took in a flying leap & then spurted a little, going straight for the Hermitage. Step by step however the King gained on him until at last not a foot intervened between the two.

Despairing of reaching the Hermitage de Smythe dropped the crown just in front of the King's feet, thus tripping him up & sending him head first, into a sandback; where he stuck head first for several minutes.

Extracting himself, the King picked the crown up & prepared to return.

This he did without accident, to his pawnshop in time for tea, and as he drank his tea he planned how he should overcome the King of Spades.

He had forgotten his encounter with the Prince Bishop so he did not notice that the body had disappeared.

CONCLUDING CHAPTER

The Prince Bishop was not quite dead & so after laying an hour or two in an insensible state he had recovered.

As soon as he was able he carefully emptied the till into his pocket and walked forth. We shall hear of him again soon.

The Desert Daisy lived a happy life with de Smythe for a month or so & then while holding a small argument with him she had tried to enforce her reasons with a broomstick.

De Smythe not being extra thick headed gave way to such forcible reasons and expired.

She died of Grief immediately after.

The People who were their neighbours (mostly Arabs) buried them in one coffin to show how inseparable they were & also because wood was rather scarce in the desert.

★ ★ ★

King Groggenose rose early the next morning & commenced raising an army to win back his kingdom.

He soon enlisted a sweeper, two or three small boys, & an elderly person of 84.

Having drilled them a little he distributed uniforms & marched. Just as he was crossing the boundary he saw someone running after him.

Telling his army to halt he waited & on the person approaching nearer he found it was 'that boy again'.

Halting a moment for that boy to fall in line, the army proceeded.

In a few minutes they were approaching the Castle of Clubs. Suddenly they saw a number of troops sallying forth from the large gate. Halting for a moment to prepare, the army advanced.

Forward they rode & Forward came the foe.

Both armys met with a crash & then all was confusion & slaughter. The Spade army being the most numerous at first appeared to gain. Headed by the King's son-in-law mounted on a towel horse & armed with a corkscrew they fought like demons.

The Victory at one time appeared certain & the Club army was only saved from defeat by the heroism of the sweep who, just as King Groggetippe was thinking of bolting, rushed into the thick of the fight & twirling himself round with his broom extended, had involved in common ruin friend & foe.

He then executed a 'pas de triumph' on the summit of the heap of struggling human beings to the intense rage of the King of Spades who mad with rage rushed downstairs (for he had been watching the battle from the clock tower) into the childrens nursery & picking thencefrom two of the chubbiest infants, he tucked one under each arm & sallied forth into the battle.

The Spades had just commenced to give way when he arrived but the unusual sight of their King armed with a couple of innocents cheered their drooping spirits.

Using the little innocents like snowballs the King dashed at his foes followed by the rest of his army. The Clubs wavered for a second time & all would soon have been lost had it not been for 'that boy' who, putting his foot out as the King of Spades rushed blindly past him, tripped the whole Charge up.

This gave the Clubs time to re-form & prepare for the final struggle.

Suddenly a cheer was heard & the King of Spades' two french cooks appeared on the scene.

The sweep was felled to the earth by a dripping pan hurled by some invisible hand.

The two or three small boys that formed the main body fiercly round the body . . . were pressed back inch by inch. All was nearly lost, when 'that glorious boy' seizing a ladle, rushed at the Spades & personally engaged the chief cook.

In a few minutes the chief cook was a lifeless corpse at his feet with the ladle run through his body. Just at this crucial juncture the Spades received a sudden reinforcement.

The Prince Bishop of Deuceace, as soon as he had been informed of the invasion of the Spades by the King of Clubs, had hurried off to take part against his rightful sovereign & arrived just as the Spades were giving way.

Cheered by this fresh addition they reformed their shattered ranks & stood ready for the final struggle. Just at this point when success was doubtful the scale was turned by a sudden & unexpected arrival.

The Commander in Chief who had been left for dead on the banks of the Duggup had in reality been only insensible & so after laying a couple of months on the field he had recovered & hurried back in time to take part in the final struggle.

Dashing into the thick of the fight he soon turned the scale. The King of Spades was sliced in half, the Prince Bishop cut in two, the King's Son in law chopped into inconcivably small bits & the second Cook banged as flat as a pancake in three seconds & ere one minute had passed the whole of the Spade army was slain & the rest fled in confusion.

The King of Clubs knighted the Commander in Chief on the spot & then marched in triumph into the Castle after giving orders for the burial of the bodys.

He increased in fame power & corpulence & lived happily ever after.

The Princess Amelia is still unmarried but there is talk about her being married soon to the Commander in Chief. I wish him joy.

Beatrix Potter 1866–1943

London

aged 13

Grandmamma Leech was telling us today about when she came to London. She did not say the date. They came up by the stage coach because great grandfather was going to buy a new one and did not wish to come in his own.

They were too many to go all at once, so great grandmamma and most of them went on in front, and grandmamma and great grandpapa followed, I suppose next day. He had been ill and grandma was to take great care of him and not to let him hang his head when he went to sleep, consequently she got no rest herself and when they stopped at an inn to eat, she begged for a bedroom where she might wash herself.

They went to Radcliffe Hotel in Blackfriar's! The fashionable place where all the Manchester people went. Great grandad was afraid to take them to the city on a weekday because of the great crowd, so he took them through Lombard Street etc. on Sunday.

He bought an immense family coach (bought of Silk's who supplied four succeeding generations), a great length with a dickie behind, two imperials on the top, large seat in front. The postillions rode the horses, of which four were necessary, a thing which greatly disturbed great grandpa, who thought it dreadful to keep so many.

They got on without mishap as far as Stockport. Great grandpa (nervous about four horses) wished to reach home after dark. The man did not know the way very well, and drove up a street which came to an end. There was the immense coach almost jambed between the houses.

A man in a nightcap put his head out of the window and exclaimed, 'What in the world have we here?' 'We may well ask what 'av we theer, but coom down an' 'elp us,' replied great grandpa. They had to pull the coach backwards, having taken out the horses, to the great amusement of the people of Stockport.

The stage coaches changed horses every ten miles and reached London in twenty-four hours. It was an excellent road. Reynolds[1] in later day rode Major up and back three times taking two days, and once when detained by a snowstorm there, three. There was one hill where outside passengers were obliged to walk up. There was a lady on the top of grandma's first journey who grumbled much at having to do it in the middle of the night.

When the railway was opened it took eight hours to come from Manchester to London. There was a certain pompous old gentleman when grandma was young who used continually to say 'I tell you some of you will see the time when one can eat one's breakfast in Manchester and one's dinner in London.' He both saw and did it himself.

When grandma was at Miss Lawrence's school, she and some other girls used occasionally to go backward and forward between Manchester and Liverpool. There was generally some gentleman going who looked after them. One day there was an old lady who was discoursing on the danger of the times, she said she was even told they were to use steam engines, she said people would be forced to travel whether they liked it or not. Mr Stuart, the gentleman, teased her finely about it.

The road from Hyde to Manchester was so bad that great grandmamma used to ride to the Assemblies on a pillion behind great grandpapa, and put on her grand dress when she got there. Some horses objected to 'double', and they always rode 'Old Jarvie'. At the bottom of the hill near the flowery field mills was a brook crossed by stepping stones which horses had to ford. One day 'Old Jarvie' was crossing carrying a 'double', when the pillion came loose and great grandma slipped over his tail into the water.

At one time there was great discontent among the mill people who were disturbed by the doctrines of a sect called Luddites, who thought everyone should be equal. They had made arrangements for a riot, decided who should be killed and how the spoil should be divided. Great grandmamma was aware that when the clothes were hung up on the lines, the mill folk decided who should have this and that. She was

[1]Their coachman.

52

Flower drawing of foxglove and periwinkle by Helen Beatrix Potter, aged nine. It is rare to find her work signed in full.

very anxious about great grandpa and wished him to go away for a bit but he wouldn't.

At last a letter was put through the hall door, informing great grandfather he was one of those to be killed, and that it was written by someone who knew what was going on. He resolved to go to Liverpool. Grandmamma who was two years old can just remember being left at her aunt's and seeing her father and mother ride off with the baby.

He was no sooner gone than there was a great clamour after him. He must come back, no one should hurt him. So in a few days he returned and things quieted down.

Grandmamma has still got her own and grandfather's wedding clothes. His were very tight-fitting. Uncle Willie tried to get them on but couldn't, which surprised grandmamma, though I should think it only natural.

Her wedding dress had very large loose sleeves with tight swansdown ones under them. People who could not afford swansdown had feathers. The sleeves were always made to take off, young ladies generally changing them in the evening, in the same way as was afterwards done with long drawers.

Mamma was once walking in the garden when a little girl, when one of the gardeners called after her that she had lost something, and presented her with an elegant embroidered drawer-leg.

Grandmamma has also a bonnet and pelisse. The bonnets had great pokes which were filled by the frills of a cap worn under them. The caps were made with great care, the great point being that they should not look prim or quakerish. The pelisse which belonged to great grandmamma is of green silk shot with blue, very pretty. It came down to the feet and had sleeves tight at the wrist and loose at the shoulder.

Grandmamma seems still to prefer post travelling for some things. She says grandfather and she drove all over England for their wedding tour in a chariot, and it was the nicest journey she ever went. Crinolines seem to have been a great trouble, particularly on tours abroad, Hannah[1] particularly disliked them. It was almost impossible to ride a mule with one on, till at last grandma found a way of tying

[1] Their old maid.

one side of the crinoline top to her waist, when she managed very nicely.

They were also worn in the mills, in spite of all that the masters could do to keep them out, for they were both in the way and dangerous.

Sunday March 12th 1882

aged 15

Wood pavement begun near Onslow Gardens Monday 6th.

There were red deer in Derbyshire at the end of the sixteenth century, their horns are to be seen in old halls.

A golden eagle built her nest in the woodlands in 1688.

They are cutting down those big trees along the road.

Minister arrived drenched. 'What shall I do, Mrs. McGregor, I'm wet through and through?' 'Get into the pulpit as fast as you can, you'll be dry enough there!'

Dr McLeod walking through the streets of Glasgow saw some little urchins playing at mud pies in the gutter. He stood behind them and asked them what they were doing, they said 'making a church', and showed him the doors, windows and pulpit, 'and where is the minister?' asked the doctor, 'Oh, we hadn't enough mud, we've sent for some more.' Some ministers are made of drier stuff than mud!

A Scotch king paying a visit to a noble family asked the lady for a toothpick after dinner. She gave him a large fish bone which *she*(!) was in the habit of using, and his majesty said his teeth were 'weel packit', which, with a fish bone, became the crest of the family.

A country man in some remote part of Scotland picked up a lobster which a fishmonger had dropped on the road. He took it to the minister of the parish who having looked in his Bible pronounced it to be either an elephant or a turtle dove.

John Gray 1866–1934

Writ by Me when I was Sixteen Years Old

The eternal dying of a summer day,
Cooled by the young moon's horizontal beams,
Lulls in that dreamy atmosphere; no sound,
Save the soft murmur of the breathing leaves,
Or the low voice of faintest cloudlets, borne
By winds so gentle that the snail's sad march
Seems as a flight precipitous to them.
There the bright spider toils with patient wreath
To close at last his geometric toil
Of centuries unnumbered. And the soul,
Clad in body sweeter, purer far,
Than on a lily's lip a drop of dew,
Drinks in the bliss unending. Peace, o peace,
After the torment of the eons, while Time's
    weary revolutions wait still to be told.

Two manuscript versions with identical words exist. Only one has the title added.

John Cowper Powys 1872–1963

Corfe Castle

aged 12

At Corfe Castle when the Shades of Night steal over the Ruins grey
There is a dungeon far from the light of day
Where now a grisly spectre holds its sway.
Among the shadowy ruins groping creeps he
And when he hears a frightful yell up leaps he
Gives such a shriek that echoes hear the sound
And make the Mighty Castle loud resound.
Then stalking slowly on in Twilight dim
He turns a corner and in front of him
He sees another spectre of the Night
A bogy that surpasses him in height.
Then there commences such a fearful fray
As ne'er was seen by the bright light of day
Then Morning breaks and both dissolve in air
And nothing's left but the Old Castle fair.

G. K. Chesterton 1874–1936

Worship

aged 16

'All thy works praise thee, O Lord'
A silence on the wooded slopes, a silence on the sea,
And would that heaven so were praised by such a peace in me,
I am a man, my heritage a curse of fire and sword,
While o'er my head the purple hills in silence praise the Lord.
From the old earth doth worship rise a hymn of ordered deeds,
But we have rent it into sects and coined it into creeds.
His myriad phrases lift their hymns in ordered calm divine,
While we must struggle for a name and slaughter for a sign.
God's solemn rocks and sunny fells their hymns are still the same;
But we have strewn them with the dead we slaughtered in His name,
And while the sweet old nature song goes up from wood and hill,
The worshippers of mortal race are madly wrangling still.
And this is he; the lord of earth, the image of the Lord,
Whose worship blasteth as a course and smiteth as a sword,
I grasp the rods and dare to claim an Eden-right divine,
To rule the living world that lifts a purer prayer than mine.
Yet lord he is, on every hand, his power is with his claim,
He rends the secret of the rocks and grasps the thunder-flame.
The cloudy confines of the earth as portals he unbars,
And tracks o'er all the silent heaven the purpose of the stars,
As a young child, mid birds and beasts with chiding and caress,
Subdues and sways their patient strength with mock imperiousness,
So mid the Titan powers of earth the child of Heaven lay,
Of wilder mood and frailer form, but loftier race than they,
While earth's mute forces blindly bent before the mystic throne,
Are conscious of a presence vague, adored but all unknown,
Man lifts a reckless gaze and strives o'er all the glimmering night,
To trace the vast unmeasured form, too awful for his sight.

Though nature's spirits lift their hymns without a doubt's alloy
From field and hill, from flower and fruit, a psalm of ordered joy,
When far behind and far below their echoes fade and die,
Goes lonely up beyond the stars the bitter human cry.
There is a place of inner life where nature cannot come,
Where in the lonely places meet the souls of God and man,
Aye, this he, the lord of earth, though lone his doom and dire,
A wild-eyed, dual mystery, a strife of dust and fire,
A flame is set upon his brow, a sword within his hand,
And on his own wild way he goes, a waster on the land.
He stirred, a far-off germ of life, at old Creation's root,
Climbed ever, with a dawning will, the cycles of the brute.
Groped blindly through unconsciousness, sought out an unknown
    goal,
And found the vision of himself, the temple of his soul.
Within that shrine a secret lies where nature has no share,
Within that shrine forever burns the mystic lamp of prayer,
In dreaming myth and frantic creed, in flame and battle-wrath,
In stormy flash and mystery, that secret goeth forth.
A glory round the wooded hills, a splendour on the sea,
And something of that sunset rest hath laid its hand on me.
Here, too, is peace, within, without, a praying world I scan
The fiery peace of eventide, the passion faith of man.

Idolatry

aged 16

Shall we turn from the mysterious dark with the pagan prayer and
    spell,
As wholly a hideous dream from the gloom of the gateway of Hell?
Shall we say of the wild-eyed savage who crouches with gibber and
    moan,
Where the dead stone god sits glaring, that the worship is dead as the
    stone?
Not so; for the worshipper lives, and with him the worship grew,

And the fear of his heart is deep and the prayer of his lips is true;
The worshipper lives and prays, and with him the worship began,
Though the fetish that towers be a fetish, the man that kneels is a man;
And a spark of the world-wide worship, dim kindled within him
  now,
Has guided the hands that fashioned and prompted the knees that
  bow.
Whence came that strange, mystical impulse, with the strength of true
  sacrifice strong,
Before symbols of earth and of heaven, before canons of right and of
  wrong?
Out of the deep, mysterious – we know not whence it began –
Yon dark barbarian, crouching with the wild and abject mien,
Is more than the sage or the prophet, the priest of the things unseen;
That groveller's wail in the darkness that rings to the silent sky
Is more than love or gospel the proof of a life on high.
Not alone to yon graven horror the man was kneeling then;
There is more than a fancy hidden in the soul of the children of men,
Not alone to you ghastly idol the savage prays today,
He prays to the presence within him that has prompted his heart to
  pray.

Edward Thomas 1878-1917

Dad

aged 16

He was a fishing acquaintance and we called him Dad. Exactly how he came to bear that name I could not tell. However that may be, from the first moment we saw and spoke to him, the name stuck where it was thrown; doubtless if we met him today Dad it would be, and Dad to the end of the chapter.

The acquaintance was made in this wise. We were roach fishing, larking about perhaps more than anything else, and could catch nothing; you see it was a scorching day and the water bright and clear as crystal. Suddenly with a tremendous stroke an old man close by threw a tiny fish up into the air and down it fell on the bordering sward. It was Dad. Up we ran to chaff him on his success – such a catch it was after nearly a whole day's ill success. Then we had a little talk, but it did not end there. Next day we met him again and shared the same swim and the same luck for we caught nothing. It was one of his good points, no amount of failure would daunt him: whether he caught little or much he was always as merry, as full of chat. Chance acquaintances like this ripened into friendship. We found he had a whole store of out of door knowledge which he was quite ready to impart.

In spite of his clothes – what difference did clothes ever make in a good strong man – he looked a finely made fellow, and we became secretly his admirers. No man at his age ever had a straighter back, that we were sure of, straight and strong it was as the ground-ash stick he always carried. His clear steel blue eyes looked you full in the face without a spark of insolence. It was a kind intelligent eye too, though he could twist a rabbit's neck on occasion with the nonchalance of a professional poacher. Time had left few furrows in that full strong face, sunburnt like his sinewy neck. His nose and chin were perhaps his strongest features; almost Grecian in their firmness and regularity.

A profusion of fair hair silver a little near the ears fell about his neck and was hardly kept back by a hard felt hat. His forehead rising from a beetling brow of dense matted hair towered with an intellectual frown. In fact his build which was sturdy and not too long, and his features not less than his manner and talk raised him above the ordinary labourer, from whose class he was sprung. He used to tell us with a sparkle of pride of enormous weights lifted by him in his youth, and of fights where he felled a man like a bullock. Recalling the mad days of youth in fact, a fierceness, almost brutal, showed itself and destroyed the symmetry of his face. In such moments he was not himself, for age had quelled the turbulant spirit, and tamed what must have been a temper indeed.

His occupation near his native village brought him into contact with the wild life of the fields, and he had not been idle in noting all he saw around him. With the ways of hares and rabbits he was familiar, and had turned his knowledge to account with the aid of a few strands of cotton wire formed into a running noose. This he taught us to manipulate, and proved its certainty with deadly accuracy by snaring a rabbit very soon after the wire was set with simple but careful judgment. The same ease and delicacy of handling was shown in wiring the long jack as they lay in the side of the brook; the reeds formed something of a screen to his movements, but were a sure warning to the pike if they rustled against his striped sides. Trout he had 'tickled' and told how he was nearly caught in the deed and to escape detection hid a wet cold trout against his bare breast under the shirt he was wearing.

The lads of the neighbourhood whence Dad hailed had a strange method of taking trout. Knowing the shyness of that fish, they arranged a mode of capture to suit his temperament. Marking a spot in the stream where a number of trout were feeding, the lads divided into two companies and entered the water on either side of the fish. Then they walked slowly towards them, beating the water and generally creating a disturbance. According to the old man's story the fish were bewildered by the number of their enemies and allowed themselves to be taken out of the water with the bare hand. Tickling trout they reduced to an art, as was necessary to circumvent so wary a fish.

But in knowledge of nature beyond that required in poaching – which is very considerable – Dad was even more erudite. He had climbed trees for the blue hawk's[1] nest, and knew its eggs and their markings; the hawfinch, that parrot of the woods with its strange cup and saucer nest was common in his time. He knew exactly where to look for the nest of any bird we were likely to come across, and by certain local circumstances was unerringly guided to a nest hidden deep perhaps in a thorn bush. There was an intricacy in his methods of discovering nests that almost amounted to casuistry and he gloried in showing his knowledge. One failing he had in common with most labourers on the soil, much inaccuracy in bird nomenclature. Thus he thought there were two distinct birds – chaffinch and pinefinch and yet called them indiscriminately twinks or pinks! The Spring imigrants were a source of much want of accuracy in this way. How to distinguish between a white-throat and a garden warbler, for instance he was at a loss, though he knew their eggs. One and all, from white-throat to chiffchaff he called 'chits' probably from their call notes. Thus cole tit and the blackcap, though he knew the chatter of the former and the wild carol of the latter, he could not distinguish and called them generally 'blackcaps'.

Birdnotes, not songs, he could imitate to the life, and had I believe made use of this faculty in trapping birds. The hollow note of the bullfinch that is almost ventriloquial in its effect, came as easily from his lips as the chuckle of a jackdaw or the chiding of a sparrowhawk at its prey. I remember being highly amused at his rendering of a young rook's cry whilst gobbling a worm: it was truly perfectly rendered. He would startle people on a dark night by making the yell of a cat. The terrified hare, tracked close by the bloodthirsty little weasel, gives out a most heartrending shriek that is almost human, this he rendered so exactly that one looked round for the victim. Such were only a few of the multitude of his accomplishments.

By pointing out a flower or describing a rarity he could make a walk supremely interesting and was indeed a charming companion on any expedition in the fields. There was not a herb or flowering plant of any sort to be met with on our walks that he did not know, and hardly one that was not invaluable as a remedy for some complaint. He certainly had no intention of allowing the old intimacy with herbs to die out. Dried specimens of many sorts he always kept by him and roots of many more. Such knowledge as he was full of is fast decaying and it is

[1]This is the West Countryman's name for a peregrine falcon.

interesting to come across this old exponent of a time-honoured homely skill. He might have made a doctor as well as a poacher.

Though the click of the neck of a rabbit under his thumb awoke no spark of pity within him after long use, there was innate love of animals which even this could not erase. Years ago he had reared several young hares by hand solely himself, and wild rabbits too, a feat this we had never heard of before. Searching the hazels in the golden woods of Autumn he had come across a creature of the woods that watched the fallen nuts. A little dormouse, helpless in his great hand that could so easily have crushed it, was taken home and cared for with animal kindness. When the family was in distress and bread was scarce, the little brown fellow never wanted for nuts. He would show you the empty kernels too, bored with a round hole as neatly as if it had been drilled, but had no explanation to offer; there seems nothing impossible in it when you see the rows of pearly teeth in the little jaw. At evening as he dozed in his straight backed chair, the pattering of tiny feet in the wooden cage above him called him for a moment from a reverie of the past to administer the creature's wants. There was a pathos about him sometimes that could not be overlooked. This is true kindness, with sacrifice and even struggling against nature – for you might see his old savagery cropping up now and then.

In modern history as it affected his class he was well informed as ever, and had a memory overflowing with detail. He was bitter against Church and State though a more truly orthodox man never breathed, and insisted that there was a separate system of law for rich and poor. When bread was a shilling a loaf and men earned less than ten shillings from a long week's work, his father or some other relation was among the most bitterly rebellious against a system that could tolerate such things. Every man poached then, and his family with the rest. He remembered hearing it said that each man in one gang at least vowed to kill or disable the keepers if they attempted to thwart their attack on the game. It was a wild time and even the old women were poachers, he said, with the aid of harmless looking dogs that barked only when they reached the cottage with a fresh killed rabbit.

Latterly Dad had sobered much when he was no longer able to perform his old feats of strength and daring. To make amends perhaps for the past he had turned tee-totaller and finally Salvationist. It was a strange step from poacher to street corner preacher, but was doubtless sincere. He was loud against 'these new religions', his woodland life and really intense sympathy with Nature could not overcome his orthodoxy, the adherence to traditional views of religion.

Myfanwy Thomas writes: 'This is Edward Thomas' adolescent description of his lifelong friend, Dad Uzzell, of Swindon. They corresponded all Edward's life, and he sent Dad his jackets and waistcoats. Dad was tremendously fond of Edwy, and wrote the most moving letters to Helen when Edward was killed. He regarded him as his own son – his own sons were bad lots and were in and out of prison, I believe. He met Dad when he spent his school holidays with his paternal grandmother – whose husband and sons had moved the family from Wales to the new railway works. Her daughters served in the station buffet.' Dad was the 'Lob' of the poem of that name.

E. M. Forster 1879–1970

The Opinions of Mistress Louisa Whichelo, The Chastiser of her Sex

aged about 12

'Here come the women! Out they walk
In groups of two and three
To chatter forth their silly talk
O'er filthy cups of tea.

'They gulp the bread and butter down
With shovellings and pecks,
They drop the jam upon their gown,
I hate the female sex.

'I hate their spaldering wet feet;
Why will they trail and roam?
If they must eat – well let them eat,
But let them eat at home.

'The proper place for womankind
Is *not* to walk outside;
But see the house is clean and mind
The men are well supplied.'

So spake Louisa, free and fair,
Yet bowed not to her rule,
For Heaven's providential care
Had classed her as a mule.

P. N. Furbank in his two volume biography of E. M. Forster (1977–8) writes: 'Guessing what lay in store for Morgan in a fatherless household, [his grandmother] formed an alliance with him against all old cats of women, with their gossip and sewing parties. . . . When he reminded her that she was a woman, she replied, "I'm not a woman, so I must be a mule".' This explains the last line of the poem. 'Spaldering' (verse 3) is a made-up adjective, suggesting probably wet feet spread out, as when fish are split open and spread out.

The Influence of Climate and Physical Conditions upon National Character

aged 16

We have so far considered the influence of nature upon races who have, so far as we know, remained in one land without emigrating during their infancy and childhood, and have therefore throughout their career been exposed to the same influences. We must next see what have been the results on those races who, having learnt the rudiments of civilization in one land, have from various causes migrated to another. If it was impossible to lay down rules for the influence of Nature on those who have always lived in the same locality, we can have little hope of finding out anything definite when speaking of those who have already acquired in their old home characteristics more or less marked, and then have migrated to a region in which they are exposed to totally different physical conditions. It is easy to see that a struggle between the man, with his half-formed mind, and the world around will inevitably ensue. Sometimes the man will win, sometimes external Nature, but more often they will each gain something, and the result will be a race which is a product of the old characteristics and the new influences. If the product is successful that race will be one of the winning nations of the world.

Let us look at the history of the Goths, one of the greatest migrating nations. By the eighth century of this era they had established themselves in Europe from Italy and Spain to France and Denmark, the northern portion living under natural conditions similar to those to which it had always been accustomed, while the southern was exposed to many new influences not the least of which was the hot sun and the climate of the south. It is the two styles of architecture whose headquarters were respectively in Normandy and at Venice that show us the mental characteristics of these two branches, and architecture inevitably shews the spirit of a nation better than literature or painting; for a picture or a book is the work of a well-educated clever man, and only represents the feelings of the highest classes of society, while a building is the work of all classes from the master-builder to the uneducated workman.

In the north the builder heaved from the mountain side masses of rock, and with them he made his church, huge, rough, irregular like one of his own cliffs, with great dark entrances like the caverns that yawned in the face of the hills. And he would not do without ornament, but hastily stuck out from rough blocks fantastic forms and grotesque shapes, such as we may see to-day in the churches of Rouen and the houses of Lisieux, not the creations of a diseased mind, like the gods of India, but the creations of a new and vigorous life. Living in the open air with much genius but with little time for thought the Northerner hastily built his church for his immediate need, and all unconsciously made it full of fire and life.

When the Goths invaded Italy they found people and art alike held by the 'golden paralysis' of Byzantium. They did not destroy the old form but breathed new spirit into it, and from the union of architectures sprang the domes of St. Mark, from the union of races the Italian nation.

Under the dreamy blue sky and amid the marble quarries they made themselves churches where men could sit and ponder, large low buildings with columns of porphyry verde and giallo, with floors of mosaic rippling like the soft Italian sea, with walls covered with Saints and Madonnas looking out of fields of blue and gold with mystic symbols – the peacock, the dove, the vine of Life, the flock of Christ, and the rivers of Paradise flowing from the foot of the Cross with stags drinking the living waters. But the formal insipidity of the Byzantine style was gone, and in its place was the living Gothic with its love of Nature which asserted itself later on in the works of Giotto, Nicolo Pisano, and Orcagna.

From this early architecture we can see the effect the climate and scenery of Italy was exerting on the Gothic mind. The dreamy beauty of the land softened the strong rough genius, and while they adopted the forms of the old civilization they filled them with new and vigorous life.

Marvellous was the influence Italy exercised over the Goths. In the course of a few centuries, without losing the national germ of energy, they were totally changed physically and mentally from the kindred races of Northern Europe, whose civilization, owing to the rough surroundings, advanced more slowly, but perhaps more surely from its very deliberation.

But if we look at the other emigrations of half-civilized races that are mentioned in history we do not always find the result we have noted above. The Moors kept their individuality in Spain, the negroes keep theirs in the United States, while on the other hand the Slavonic invaders of Greece have been completely absorbed by the indigenous inhabitants, so that the present nation still possesses in a marked degree the characteristics of ancient Hellas.

We have traced the influence of Nature on savages and on semi-civilized nations, and have seen that in the case of emigration a struggle takes place between the man and his new surroundings. Now, before concluding, we must briefly touch upon the influence of change of climate and locality on a highly civilized race. We find the influence is very little, sometimes hardly perceptible. An Englishman is an Englishman, whether he is on the plains of South Africa or the mountains of Upper India, and though his descendants live in these places for hundreds of years they will never in the slightest degree resemble Hottentots or Chitralis. The reason of this is that the civilized world has gained individuality. In the great struggle between man and his surroundings, man has now the upper hand. Aided by modern science he can to a great extent make Nature subservient to his will instead of being moulded to hers.

We have now finished our brief survey of the influence natural laws exercise on the characteristics of the human race, an influence sometimes ignored, sometimes exaggerated, but of which, even in this age of scientific discovery, no one can form a due estimate. It is impossible to lay down a definite rule, and we can only compare examples which often seem to prove facts totally at variance with each other, and we must leave to future generations the solution of this great problem, and the discovery of the hidden laws that link together in inextricable union the workings of Nature and the fortunes of man.

Wyndham Lewis 1882–1957

Good Times

aged 10

'So it is' said I.

'All hands shorten sail' shouted Mortar.

There was a great hubub in which I had a good share.

'Now boys lower the dinghy and Charlie do you think you could get in and steer, and have Brown, Donagan and Hayward in with you to row' said Mortar.

'Obey orders, sir' said I.

The real force of the storm had abated, and [in] thick mist [only a] gusty wind made the sloop go. Now getting into the dinghy and rowing or sailing about was a very simple thing. We rowed away from the sloop into the darkness, and soon saw something black looming ahead.

We all ready felt the impulse of the surf but rowed on, now at the top of a surging breaker, now in a hollow of foaming water, drenched to the skin and our boat half full of water we ran up a little river or creek only about 14 ft. wide and rather shallow, just allowing our boat to go on easyly. It was evidently a tropical place but more astounding still quite light with the moon and stars.

Hayward jumped from the boat, made it fast and commenced violently to shake a cocoanut palm that stood near by.

I jumped out the other side and wandered about. I was walking near the sound and had just walked down to it when I utered a cry and stood tranfixed.

For there before me all over cinders was a human skeleton, bound to a tree, and a fire still smouldering underneath it and by its side. As well as this, naked footmarks in great number marked the sands.

Seeing the footmarks were not recently made, I stumbled rather than walked through the darkness of the jungle, which the moon or stars did not penetrate, to the top of a hill and I was awestruck with the magnificance of the cenery and said at the same time,

'I am monarch of all I survey
My right there is none to dispute
From the centre all round to the sea
I am lord of the foul and the brute.
O solitude where are the charms,
That sages have seen in thy face?
Better dwell in the midst of alarms
Than reign in this horible place!'[1]

'That's too true lad, I am allso a spectator of this magnificent sene' said a low, deep ernest voice. I turned round in an instant and saw before me a man in the skins of beasts.

There I stood in an attitude of defence, a club in one hand, a revolver in the other.

'Ah boy, where have you been wrecked?' said the man.

'Well I am not wrecked, but just come ashore to look about, but whom are you may I ask?' I said.

'I am a castaway sailor, I have been on this desolate Isle for nearly twenty years, and I am constantly desterbed by wild savages, canibals, who come over every two months' said the man.

'We are all armed and are going to stay here a short time and then take you off with us now –'

'What's the matter lad?' said the man.

'I heard a faint yell and – Look there!' said I.

The little creek ended at the foot of the hill and the other three boys had rowed to the foot of the hill, (as I was afterwards told) and had just reached the bottom when a naked warrior with feathers, shield and spear went rushing away with a fierce yell of defiance.

At the same time Brown seemed to rise from the ground in front of the wild savage.

I was now an eyewitness to the sene. Brown was carrying cocoanuts, but at seeing the wild figure dashing towards him, instead of taking to his heals, he droped the cocoanuts, and calmly drew his cutlass (that had been lent to him) and held it aloft in both hands.

In the midst of all the excitement there was a report, the canibal threw his hands up in the air with a piercing yell, and reeled forward. It

[1]William Cowper, attributed to Alexander Selkirk (1782).

was Hayward that had fired. Hayward fired his revolver in despair, thinking it would not go off. Just then the stillness was broken by a vivid flash of lightning, and a gust of wind (for after all the yelling and firing, the world –

'a sudden stillness held').

We all stood togeather, us for[1] boys and the castaway. Just then there was a faint report and a milk white star illuminated the sky.

We left the Indian and sprang into the boat, and well for us we had, for the earth seemed to shake with the trampling of feet and the fierce warcries of savages.

'Row for your lives boys, row for your lives' said the man, setting the example.

'What is your name, sir?' said Donagan, for we were quite convinced he was a thorough gentleman by now.

'Call me Johnson the Castaway' he said rather sadly.

Another rock – and another, and another. 'Did you hear the boom of a gun just then, Charlie' said Donagan.

'Yes, Halloa. Look there on the reefs or shore or sands, it – there goes a rocket, and I'm bothered if [the sloop] is not wrecked' said I.

We soon reached her and told all that had hapened to us. It seemed that the crew (Mortar, Frank, Lincon, Alderman and Deen) had got anxious about us and put close in shore. They sent up the first rocket, and at the same time a tremendous squall, and a flash of lightning sent them on the reefs. They then sent up more rockets and at last [fired] their little cannon. That night we sent out scouts (for the rest of the night) and kept sentinels as well.

In the morning our guest came forward as different as a man could be.

There was only a board or two gone, and the sloop could easily be put right again. She was wedged in among two big rocks and stood upright. We slept in her that night and our guest found a razor and a suit of the Captain's clothes. The morning was beautiful and the sun and breezs were refreshing, all the black fog having cleared away. But the highest tide in the Island could not reach our boat, [since she] had been carried up by a tremendous breaker.

[1]four.

Our guest came down in clothes and appearance of a man of 35 years.

But he was not perfect yet. After breakfast he went to his cabin and came out in different clothes and only a mustash, not as before with only half his beard cut off. Soon the scouts came in numbering 2, but the third did not return. It was Mortar, one of the Chief's boys. The time passed on and Frank one of the sentinels was found missing. But our anxiety did not last long. They both came back in a great hurry, saying that on a little hill not far from us [they] could see the natives in full warpaint. We all hurried to the top of the hill and in mid ocean we saw hundreds of canoes heading away. Through my glass I could see one canoe very plainly and evidently it was a Chief's canoe.

We all went back and then went into the Island about a mile and cut down the trees for about half a mile and then returned to the boat. In a week we had made a large playground for sports and games.

We now began the building of a house or fort by the playground. In a month it was finished and a high palisade of 10 feet was built around it with the little cannon pointing out. All arms and tools and clothing and gardening and everything was kept in there. We lived in it.

One day we were all strolling on the sands, when Johnson drew me aside, and said 'Now lad, you won't blab if I tell you something.'

'Of course not, sir' I replied.

'You think my name is Johnson, but I am really Sir Edward More, the explorer, and while on my voyage to South America I was wrecked' said the man.

'You! Are the great explorer?' I exclaimed.

'Ay, Ay lad, I am. But I brought you here for other things. At this very moment three thousand savages are encamped!'

'Tell the other fellows then, quick!' said I.

'Cooly, cooly lad, go tell them all to tarry here.'

I ran with all my might, and we were soon all assembled (except Mortar). We did not notice it at first but after a while Mortar was called upon to give his opinion.

'Where is Mortar?' was the general cry.

'Here' said Mortar stepping out of the bushes. 'I have seen thousands of natives, they are on the move.'

'Now lads, don't get excited, be as cool as Mortar and you'l do' said Johnson. 'In future call me Sir Edward.'

pointing out, all arms
and tolls and clothing
and gardening and
everything was kept in
there. We lived in it.

One day we were all strolling
on the sands, when Johnson
drew we aside, and said
" now lad, you wont blab if
I tell you something".
"Of course not, sir " I replied
" You think my name is
Johnson, but I am realy
Sir Edward More, the

Charlie (alias Percy Wyndham Lewis) with the explorer Sir Edward More inside the fort which they built on the island (left), and (right) 'strolling on the sands' with Sir Edward.

explorer, and while on my
voyage to south America
I was wrecked." Said the man.

"You! are you the Great explorer."
I exclaimed.
"Ay, ay lad, I am. But I
brought you here for
other things. At this very
moment three thousand
savages are encamped!".
"Tell the other fellows then,

Just then Donagan fired one of his pistols. It was the first time he had fired since we had been on the Island.

'Now boys to our fort' said Sir Edward.

We rushed into the fort and shut the gate.

We loaded the cannon and our rifles, hauled up the flag and made other preparations for the defence. In two hours we heard the yells of the savages. And in another quarter-of-an-hour saw them in full warpaint. They came on in a surging mass, but stoped abruptly on seeing us. Their Chief advanced, and said something in his own language.

He returned again and directly afterwards a score of spears and arrows came dashing in upon us.

Then came the word –

'Ready! Present! Fire!!!'

At the same time the cannon thundered out, and sent destruction into the midst of the enemy. The seige continued the same for three days, sometimes the Indians would make a rush, but allways retreat again in the end. The third day a very serious conversation ensued.

'Now Sir Edward I have found the water is running short' said Lincon.

'Ay lad, I am affraid it is' said Sir Edward.

'Well, after supper tonight it will be all gone.'

'Yes lad, quite so. It is impossible to hold out without water.'

'But how is it its gone?' said I.

'Goodness-knows. I am sure I do not' said Alderman.

The next day we did without water, the second we got awfully thirsty, and the third [we] were almost dead. On that day Mortar was missing too, and was found insencible on the ground. The savages now made furious attacks.

Next morning Frank and I were on watch, when a terrible rush was made, and before we could repell it the gate was dashed open and all of us had to flee to the house. On came the wild canibals in a headlong rush, and we fought with cutlass, knife and the butt end of our rifles. Lincon was knocked down insencible, and Hayward slightly wounded. Deen flourished his cutlass with great energy, yelling all the time.

Just then a large lankey looking savage came up to me, raised his club and in a minute I would have fallen for ever, had not a thunderous roar, and a great shot come crashing through the building, and swept

the natives away with it. Then roar after roar and shot after shot came crashing over the Island.

The natives fled to the other side of the Island where their canoes were. We went on the beach and saw a cloud of smoke on the sea and the British ensign.

We cheered, and, we cheered and cheered.

O Fons Bandusiae

aged about 15

Brighter than glass Bandusian spring
  For mellow wine and flowers meet,
The morrow thee a kid shall bring
  Boding of rivalry and sweet
Love in his swelling forms. In vain
He, wanton offspring, deep shall stain
Thy clear cold streams with crimson rain.

The raging dog star's season thou,
  Still safe from in the heat of day,
When oxen weary of the plough
  Yieldst thankful cool for hers that stray.
Be of the noble founts! I sing
The oak tree o'er thine echoing
Crags, thy waters murmuring.

Virginia Woolf 1882–1941

Love-Letters between Fanny Smith and John Lovegate

aged 9

(He) My own sweet Love

My heart is so full that I feel I cannot express my sentiments with mere pen and ink but I will at least make a poor endeavour. As I gaze upon thy sweet face I see with what condescending grace You look upon your humble lover. And I give him many a qualm to suffer.

I hope my own dearest that you do not intend to make me suffer for if you do I feel that it is too much for human nature to bear. I went to a party at Mrs Robinson's where as she told me she had selected the most charming girls she could but not one of them was a quarter so charming as my own darling Fanny. I danced with a girl who was high upon aristocrats but who did not speak with half the fluency or originality of my own true love. Do not leave me in suspense any longer my darling for who but the lover can know what a terrible pain that leaves gnawing at his heart.

Adieu! adieu! oh fondly loved maiden.

Your own

John

(She) My own dearest John

How can you for one moment doubt my affections? They are so great that sickness pain or seperation cannot remove them.

I must however first ask my parents leave to marry you.

Until them I remain

your own

most loving

Fanny

At the top of these letters Virginia Woolf wrote: 'These love-letters are to show young people the right way to express what is in their hearts.'

To the Light-House

On Saturday morning Master Hilary Hunt and Master Basil Smith came up to Talland House and asked Master Thoby and Miss Virginia Stephen to accompany them to the light-house as Freeman the boatman said that there was a perfect tide and wind for going there. Master Adrian Stephen was much disappointed at not being allowed to go. On arriving at the light-house Miss Virginia Stephen saw a small and dilapidated bird standing on one leg on the light-house. Mrs Hunt called the man and asked him how it had got there. He said that it had been blown there and they then saw that it's eyes had been picked out. On the way home Master Basil Smith 'spued like fury'.

Miss Smith

aged 12

From her infancy upwards Miss Smith had known that she was remarkable. She had been once upon a time the most remarkable baby ever known, and as she became older her intellect surprised her more and more. At 12 she delighted in Virgil, at 14 she wrote sonnets, at 16 she declared that life was not worth living and retired from the world. To a young lady of such an impressionable nature these accomplishments could not but prove what an exceptional person Miss Smith was. When she appeared in society as she did at the age of 20, her curiosity to see the world having overcome her contempt of it, she protested that society must be entirely reorganised. The position of men and women towards each other was altogether disgraceful. She wrote the most remarkable essays upon Women's Rights, and declared herself to be a temperance lecturer. She had determined that men were brutes and the only thing that women could do was to fight against them. She was with ladies a good natured, conceited girl. When a man approached she stuck out her bristles like a porcupine, and made herself as disagreeable as possible. She had believed that the world would stop still and look at her, and that if she was not applauded, at any rate she would create a stir and a bustle and a confusion. Her disappointment was sincere and deep when she discovered that no one took much notice of her. Men disliked her and women tolerated her as plain and ordinary. At 30 she had deserted Woman's Rights and Temperance [and] was settling down into a mild hobly. She thought bitterly of her former self and prepared to live her life alone. It was just about this time, when she had with many pangs allowed herself to be only a woman, that a gallant gentleman appeared, and so lonely had Miss Smith become, and so much did she feel the need of someone stronger and wiser than herself that she consented to become his wife. So the two married like ordinary human beings, and she proved to be an excellent wife, and later on a devoted mother.

Anna Wickham 1884–1947

The Man in the Moon

aged 16

The man in the moon made love to the sea,
And he breathed his love to the midnight air,
And he whispered, 'Dear one, lovest thou me?'
As he stooped to kiss her seaweed hair.

Ah, she knew not then that his heart was cold,
And her bosom heaved with a happy sigh,
'I have loved you dear, with a love untold,
That will not change and cannot die.'

Then the man in the moon was up and away,
And off to the sky with a mocking shout;
But the faithful sea from that dreary day
Has followed him sighing the world about.

In Anna Wickham's play *The Seasons*, described as 'a speaking tableau for girls', this poem is spoken by the character referred to as 'a Wave of the Sea'. The play was published privately under the author's maiden name of Edith Harper. It was written for the children, parents and staff of the school at which she worked in Sydney, Australia, at the turn of the century. It involved a hundred performers.

Andrew Young 1885–1971

Battle of Bannockburn

aged 5

They fell, they fell
Till there were few to tell
How the great battle was ended.

Ezra Pound 1885–1972

Limerick

aged 11

There was a young man from the West,
He did what he could for what he thought best;
   But election came round;
   He found himself drowned,
And the papers will tell you the rest.

Pound's first published poem was this limerick, which appeared in the *Jenkinstown Times–Chronicle* on 7 November 1896. It concerns the defeat at the local Philadelphia polls of Williams Jennings Bryan, a fanatical defender of religious fundamentalism.

Siegfried Sassoon 1886–1967

Something about Myself

aged 11

Of course it isn't of any consequence but it might be of some use to tell you about myself, and how I came to be what I am. I might have told you before that I'm very well bred for one thing: and very beautiful for another, though perhaps I can't exactly say my mother was, and a greater part of her relations are most decidedly common, if not vulgar; and as her great grandfather abided among the lonely chimney-pots of London, I can't exactly call my decent[1] illustrious, in spite of my great beauty. Some cats say that I am cocky, but I can't see any harm in righteous pride.

My two brothers (both of whom disappeared in wicker-baskets) weren't exactly ugly, though, as my mother says I'm of rather a critical disposition. I expect if they had been my cousins, I should have considered them decidedly plain, but as it is, I should think they were rather pretty, though of course, not so perfectly exquisite as myself.

Well myself and my mother lived in a little hollow on a huge wall, covered with moss and lichen and nearly overgrown with ivy, and if I looked out, I could see all the people on the lawn walking about on their hind legs, purring in loud voices much louder than I ever purr, though my mother does say my purr is really remarkable for its loudness. I've heard that my mother's swearing is exceptionally loud, and my Uncle Tim, who is the biggest poacher in these parts, says that my swearing is very good for a kitten of my age, which I consider a highly flavoured compliment. I might also tell you that my uncle is a professor in the noble art of snarling, and he practises for an hour daily on two young kittens kept for the purpose, and he says he is going to teach me some day.

You see that in the picture[2] my uncle is holding up one of his hind-

[1]decent=descent. [2]Lost.

legs as if to scratch himself, but you have noticed that just behind him there is another cat, and if he were angry with that cat, he would turn round, lift up one leg, spin round again on the other, and give forth a most effectual exhibition of snarling. I only hope he'll include the figure in my lessons.

Well on the day when I begin my story my mother announced to me the awful news that three great vulgar cats had come into the garden with the intention of sweeping both me and my mother clear off the face of the earth, though I never did know that it had got one. 'Pist, quack, fiz, grrrh!!!!' These were the sounds that came upon my ears. Plucking up courage I cleared a big ivy leaf aside and looked out. The moon was full up and lit up the whole lawn brilliantly. But I hadn't time to take the scene in, for there in the middle of the lawn were three enormous cats. Tim and my mother were facing them, and the five of them were indulging in snarls and cusses of a base key. I hesitated, but only for a moment and spitting with all my might, I sprang out and bounded across the lawn. In a moment I found there was a large tabby cat sitting on my chest – glaring at me. 'Ya' a' a' was all I could say, for in another moment another cat came rushing along and began pommeling me. 'Oh my ears and whiskers! pssha sssh!' I exclaimed, and after a desperate struggle I unseated my oponent and dashed into the bushes, climbed a laurel bush and remained there. After a while, one by one, those vulgar cats dissapeared, and at last I was alone.

So I commenced singing a song in a minor key. Suddenly I heard someone coming and it was my uncle. 'Hullo' he ejaculated. 'Frrrrol, ffreela, freeli, froolerun, froleree,' I sang. 'Come down from there, or I'll fetch you down,' he said sternly. So I descended. He led me away under a tree, and there lay my mother; as dead as a doornail.

'That finishes the old gal,' I remarked gaily, for I never did like her pitucularly. But here I must end my Story, for my uncle is going to give me a snarling lesson. Though, I might tell you, I am a kitchen cat now, and catch a lot of mice.

In the Churchyard

aged 11

The chapel walls were moulded and decayed.
Within great men had been for ever laid.
Each with his head on pillowing stone, reposed,
With his hands uplifted and his eyelids closed.
   Let me not enter in the dark night hours
   Lest they should wake and walk and live like men.

Ronald Firbank 1886–1926

From *Lila*

aged 10

'. . . d'you do, who would have [fancied] seeing you here, I thought you were still away.' She spoke in a drawl, trying to quiet a rigling lap dog which she was holding in her arms. We returned last week, Lila said & have been staying with some friends of Lady Barchester's in Wales. Wales is charming said Mrs Keston, squesing her dog who was making overtuers to Lila's retriever who was laying peaceably on the mat. I've just been over to the Swintons with a message from my husband. May I perswade you to come & have lunch with me Miss Rivers, I'me all alone! Lila hesitated I am afraid – she began. You will come? said Mrs Keston perswasifley. I am *so* dreadfully dull, Harry (aluding to her husband) has gone rabbit shooting & wont be back until seven. So Lila consented, & sent word by a village child to Lady Bonchester saying that she would not be back till after lunch, the dog she left with the post mistress until she returned. Mrs Keston swept out of the post office after sending a telegram & Lila followed not sorry to have at last something to do. Mrs Keston talked nonsense the whole time, hardly giving Lila time to answer they passed up the drive to the house, it was a lovely old place sairounded by a park filed with beautiful trees, which was in full sight of the sea. They went into the dining room, Mrs Keston put the dog in its basket, tited her hair before a mirror, langwidly sat down & calved a chicken. She asked the butler when the master would be home, & then began chattering away to Lila. It was so funney she said, when I was staying with my sister we drove one morning to see a cousin of ours who is at a small girls school, we were asked to stay for lunch. Miss Raymer the head mistress asked Rachel why she did not eat her beef, & on being told that she did not care for it underdone, Miss Raymer grew angry & said, waste not want not, & eat it up, but Rachel tossed her head. I have quite good enough blood in my family without going to a bullock for

more, she said leaving the room & slaming the door & what did Miss
Raymer say laughed Lila. She said she was 'excessifley vulger' & gave
us a lecture on the decay of modern manners.

The Wind & the Roses

aged 16

Poor pale Pierrot, through the dark boughs peering
In the purple gloaming of a summers evening –
Oh! his heart is bleeding, can't you hear him sobing?
Or is it the wind that's sighing amongst the yellow roses?

Hush! . . .

Tis the wind that's sighing amongst the yellow roses.

Wrapped in bluest shadow, poor Pierrot hiding
Sees the faithless Pierrette for her lover waiting
She sits by a fountain in an Italian Garden
And her tiny hands are full of scarlet Tulips.

'Neath the dark boughs Pierrot, for the moon is waiting.
He can see the sky like the blue sea dreaming
And a great gold cloud like a net is gleaming
An amber lure for silver fishes –

Then near at hand a voice starts singing,
And a harp like a soul in love sounds throbing
Through the turquoise air –
And amidst the boughs poor Pierrot spying, sees Colombine draw
    near.

Tall Colombine through the waving roses
That cling about him like pale faces
Crushes beneath his satin slippers
The red orlanders, and the sleeping violets –

Pierrette, smiling at her mirror, sees her lover's form reflected
All amongst the cloud white roses –
Then letting fall her scarlet tulips, she trips amongst the bleeding
    Fuschias
And embraces Colombine with many kisses –

Poor pale Pierrot, through the dark boughs peering
Hears the kisses of his own dear love one
And his heart now sore, & quite, quite broken
He stabs himself with a silver dagger –

Far away in the country dreary
The blue hills, 'neath the round moon weary
Seem lost in thought –

Hush! . . .

On a green bough bending
A nightingale is sobing
Out a tale of love –

See! the grey light dawning
Pierrette has found Pierrot lying
With a knife in his heart.

Hush! . . . is she crying . . . ?

No . . . Tis only the wind that's sighing
Amongst the yellow roses.

When Firbank discovered *Lila* among his mother's papers in June 1925 he wrote to
Carl van Vechten that he was glad that he had had 'the tact not to rush headlong into
print'. Some lines from 'The Wind & the Roses' are included in *Vainglory* (1915),
where they are attributed to a woman poet who attempts to 'out-Chatterton
Chatterton'. However, at the time that he wrote the poem he thought highly enough
of it to sign it and give it to his mother for safekeeping.

T. E. Lawrence 1888–1935

Playground Football

aged 16

As there does not appear to be any handbook published on playground football, a few words on the subject will be appropriate. The game consists of two sides; and any number may play on each side; also any number may belong to neither side; in fact most belong to no side, but are free agents: this is one advantage of the game, for if you are a free agent you may suppose yourself on which side you like. At first sight it would seem to be drawback; one wouldn't know which way to kick the ball; but – and this is one point in which 'Playground Football' differs from ordinary football – we do not score by goals. As a matter of fact there seems to be only one goal in the place where we play the game, so that it would be rather difficult to know whose goal it was. The chief way to score is to kick the ball against a window; this scores the price of the window. It is rather expensive to be a good player. The method of play is entirely different from ordinary football, although that may seen a trivial matter to some. It is not necessary to kick the ball; you can kick any one else; it will do just as well, unless they are bigger than you, but there you have to take your chance. I should like to pass a few remarks on the ball. When I say 'ball', I don't necessarily mean 'ball': a ball is not at all necessary; a stone or a cap (someone else's for preference) will do as well. The only indispensable adjunct is the playground; you must have that. I believe there is a proverb somewhere about a rolling stone gathering no moss; I am quite sure a rolling football gathers a lot of mud. When a football is done with, the mud might be used to plant a flower-garden round the playground. One could make a nice lot of statistics out of playground football. For instance, if all the mud were scraped off a football in a year it would make a mountain as high as Mt. Shotover. All the force used in a year to kick a football would be given off in a millenium by £5,000 worth of radium or in 5 minutes by two people discussing the fiscal question.

Now that I have started talking about radium, I have a question for the scientific, 'why does the ball always seem to be attracted by corners in the playground?' For instance, you will see in some corner a little group of boys discussing the fiscal question or attending to their 'Little Maries'; up comes the ball, and, depositing a quantity of its superfluous mud where it is not required, knocks someone in the face; then someone will cry out 'Hands', or 'who told you to kick the ball?' Then before they have picked themselves up and repaired the damaged portions of their anatomy, the ball rolls off merrily to jump over the wall into someone else's back garden. So it keeps on, ever rolling, until the bell rings and all is done.

Playground Cricket

aged 16

Playground cricket has no handbook, so I think that some hints to youngsters who aspire to gain honours in this subject will be acceptable. The game runs on slightly the same ground as Playground Football, so that there must be some likeness between their respective implements. A playground is again indispensable, but a cap will not do for the ball. It can however be a stone, or a piece of wood: I have even seen a potato used with success. One man bats, another forty or so bowl. There are generally two balls, which are committed to the safe keeping of the Captain during school hours. The forty boys scrimmage for the balls, and a game of Rugby football is played, till one gets hold of it and bowls at the stumps. The stumps deserve mention. A wooden wall was improvised for wicket-keeper, and 3 stumps were chalked upon it, in white and blue. These having slightly faded a second pair in white was applied to the first, coinciding in width but not in height; consequently six inches of blue overtop the white bails. The profound wisdom which dictated this may not appear at first sight, but the fact is that when big boys are bowling the blue is counted as the top; when big boys are batting the stumps do not extend beyond the white. That shows our wisdom. Unfortunately some facetious individual (we would duck him if we could find him) has added four more white stumps, and four more bails, which slightly disconcert the batsmen, but greatly improve the chances of the bowler.

The block is the next matter of importance. It can be located anywhere within the four mile radius, but on this occasion is about three feet away from the stumps, and bears about 45° E. of N. from a straight line drawn at right angles to the stumps. The block itself is an irregular shaped opening resembling the Isle of Wight, 263 centimetres in length, and from 8 to 5 centimetres in width, in depth about 10 centimetres. The bat is indescribable. A mass of willow, slightly rotten in places, and resembling a mop at the bottom. The handle is said to be cane, but one player who has had a most extensive and varied acquaintance with canes, both at home and abroad, declares that no cane *ever* stung like this bat, so it must be of some foreign substance. The balls go, some into the side windows of the school, some through those of the factory, others again attach themselves to the windows opposite.

T. S. Eliot 1888–1965

A Lyric

aged 16

If Time and Space, as Sages say,
　　Are things which cannot be,
The sun which does not feel decay
　　No greater is than we.
So why, Love, should we ever pray
　　To live a century?
The butterfly that lives a day
　　Has lived eternity.

The flowers I gave thee when the dew
　　Was trembling on the vine,
Were withered ere the wild bee flew
　　To suck the eglantine.
So let us haste to pluck anew
　　Nor mourn to see them pine,
And though our days of love be few
　　Yet let them be divine.

The Man who was King

aged 16

Cap'n Jimmy Magruder, retired A.B. mariner, and at present engaged in lobster-trawling and skippering summer visitors, is famous in his own country for his genius at telling stories of his adventures at sea. There is one in particular of his brief experience as a king of which he is particularly fond. I have heard him tell it many times, and always with different and more wonderful incidents. The main facts, however, which he includes in every edition, are like this.

One cruise he was on a sailing vessel in Polynesia. The ship, an old one, went to pieces in a storm, about latitude 22 degrees, south. I never could find out anything certain about this shipwreck, but it is certain that after the boat went down the captain found himself clinging to a spar, with nothing in sight but a low-lying island about half a mile away, and the reef, boiling with breakers, on which the ship had split. To this island he slowly made his way, holding on to the gaff, and was finally flung half-drowned upon the long sandy beach.

This island, he found out afterwards, was Matahiva, in the Paumota group. Not long after the captain was there, the French got hold of it and built a post there. They educated the natives to wear clothes on Sunday and go to church, so that now they are quite civilized and uninteresting. But till the day when the captain was thrown on the beach, a white man had never been there, which was the reason he was received with so much honour.

The captain crept into a dense thicket of tari-bushes and fell sound asleep. It was several hours before he awoke, to find himself in a rather unusual position. He was being borne on a kind of litter by two of the islanders, and formed a part of a procession. First marched along the path two natives, who seemed to be priests, by their having more clothes than the rest, and carrying bowls filled with smoking incense, which had a most unpleasant odour. Next came the two men with the litter and after that a little mob of men beating bhghons (a sort of cross between tin pan and gong) and chanting monotonously.

The captain of course did not understand all this, but learned of it afterwards. It appears that the king had just died, and that while they were casting about for a new one, somebody discovered the captain asleep on the shore. As he was strangely dressed and moreover, of a whitish colour, they straightway concluded that the gods had dropped him down for the purpose of ruling over them, and were now triumphantly bearing him to the village to inaugurate him.

The captain soon found out that instead of being about to be roasted for the consumption of his hosts, he had attained a position of greater importance than he had ever aspired to reach. He succeeded to all the positions of the late monarch, including a royal palace, which was about the size of a large woodshed, and was considered something remarkable by his subjects, the royal harem, and the royal fishing boat, which was at least two feet longer than any other on the island. Life consisted of fishing, bathing, feasting and getting drunk on wine made of madu-nut.

He ruled in this way for several months, and would have stayed there for the rest of his life, had not a rebellion arisen. The cause was this, the former king had been in the custom of performing magic at the public festivals, such as breathing fire, holding a red-hot iron, or vanishing into the air on an endless rope, thereby earning great respect and admiration of his subjects. The captain could do none of these things: at feasts he only got drunk, which was not a remarkable enough feat to excite applause. Of this plot against him he was informed by a trusty slave, who crept into his palace in the night. He at once went down to the shore and, stocking his boat with provisions, set out without delay. His objective point was Tahiti, which is about three hundred miles away. Having a fair breeze and good weather all the way, he reached Tahiti in about two weeks from the time of setting out.

Katherine Mansfield 1888–1923

The Sea

aged 14

O the beauty, O the grandeur of the sea
What stories does its changeful visage tell
To you and me.

When fiercely rage the tempests o'er the deep
And all the slumb'ring world is waked from sleep
When the sea sobs, as if in sad distress
And none are there to cheer my lonliness
I feel for thee O Sea.

In calm and Tempest and in storm and strife
In all the bitter changeful scenes of life
In death's dark hour before Eternity
I feel for thee, O Sea.

The Three Monarchs

aged 14

Day took off her azure mantle
She laid down her golden crown
And she sank to her rest on the cloudlets
On pillows of rosy down.

Twilight, clad in a sombre mantle
Ascended the vacant throne
His face was haggard and weary
And his courtiers left him alone.

When the reign of Twilight was over
Night, clad in a robe of black
Saw the far away form of the monarch
And beckoned to him to come back.

But Twilight, his course pursuing
Ne'er turned, ne'er lifted his head
And the face of Night grew despairing
In low hollow tones he said

'Alas! Alas! where are my brethren?
Am I left here alone to die?
Does no one care for my welfare
When I on my deathbed lie?'

And he wrapt his robe around him
And down in the darkness he lay
The reign of the Night was over
And back to her throne came Day.

In the Tropics

aged 14

How I love to wake in the morning
And know I am far out at sea
That night has gone, day is dawning
And I am with thee, with thee.

And I go out on deck in the sunshine
And the sea is as calm as a lake
See the flying fish far on the starboard
There is no sound the silence to break.

Save the lazy flap-flap of the mainsail
And the voice of the men at their tasks –
O Sea, how I love to be with thee
'Tis all that my tired spirit asks.

And we pace the ship, forard in silence
Your hand clasped in mine, and our eyes
Gaze up far on the distant horizon
To the place our future home lies.

And at night, when the stars come out slowly
And we glide ever on in the dark
And the phosphorus floods past like fireballs
There is no sound our silence to mark.

O the peace, and the hush, and the beauty
I would that my sea life would last
And I left all my Soul in the Tropics
And my heart 'tis bound up in the past.

W. N. P. Barbellion 1889–1919

The Naturalist

aged 13

I was glad yesterday to see the egg season so well in. I shall have to get blow-pipes and egg drills. Spring has really arrived and even the grasshoppers are beginning to stridulate, yet Burke describes these little creatures as being 'loud and troublesome' and the chirp unpleasant. Like Samuel Johnson, he must have preferred brick walls to green hedges. Many people go for a walk and yet are unable to admire Nature simply because their power of observation is untrained. Of course some are not suited to the study at all and do not trouble themselves about it. In that case they should not talk of what they do not understand. . . . I might have noticed that I have used the term 'Study of Nature'. But it cannot be called a *study*. It is a pastime of sheer delight, with naught but beautiful dreams and lovely thoughts, where we are urged forward by the fact that we are in God's world which He made for us to be our comfort in time of trouble. . . . Language can express the joy and happy forgetfulness during a ramble in the country. I do not mean that all the ins and outs and exact knowledge of a naturalist are necessary to produce such delight, but merely the common objects – Sun, Thrush, Grasshopper, Primrose, and Dew.

Squirrels

aged 14

Went out with L— to try to see the Squirrels again. We could not find one and were just wondering if we should draw a blank when L— noticed one clinging to the bark of a tree with a nut in its mouth. We gave it a good chase, but it escaped into the thickest part of the fir tree, still carrying the nut, and we gave up firing at it. Later on, L— got foolishly mischievous – owing, I suppose, to our lack of sport – and unhinged a gate which he carried two yards into a copse, and threw it on the ground. Just then, he saw the Squirrel again and jumped over the hedge into the copse, chasing it from tree to tree with his catty. Having lost it, he climbed a fir tree and sat there on the tree top, and I, below, was just going to lift the gate back when I looked up and saw a farmer watching me, menacing and silent. I promptly dropped the gate and fled. L— from his Squirrel's drey, not knowing what had happened, called out to me about the nest – that there was nothing in it. The man looked up and asked him who he was and who I was. L— would not say and would not come down. The farmer said he would come up. L— answered that if he did he would 'gob' on him. Eventually L— climbed down and asked the farmer for a glass of cider. The latter gave him his boot and L— ran away.

Wild Duck

aged 16

Went to F— Duckponds. Flocks of Wigeon and Teal on the water. Taking advantage of a dip in the land managed to stalk them splendidly, and for quite a long time I lay among the long grass watching them through my field-glasses. But during the day Wild Duck are not particularly lively or interesting birds. They just rest serenely on the water like floating corks on a sheet of glass. Occasionally one will paddle around lazily. But for the most part they show a great ennui and seem so sleepy and tired that one would almost think to be able to approach and feed them out of the hand. But I moved one hand carelessly and the whole flock was up in a minute and whizzing across the river. Afterwards, at dusk, on returning to the ponds, they had come back; but now that the sun was down, those dozy, flapdoodle creatures of the afternoon were transformed into quacking, quarrelsome, blustering birds that squabbled and chivvied each other, every moment seizing the chance of a luxurious dip, flinging the ice-cold water off their backs with a shake of the tail that seemed to indicate the keenest-edged delight.

It was now quite dark. A Snipe rose at my feet and disappeared into the darkness, Coots and Moorhens clekked, and a Little Grebe grew bold and began to dive and fish quite close to me, methodically working its way upstream and so quartering out its feeding area.

A happy half-hour! Alas! I enjoy these moments the more as they recede. Not often do I realise the living present. That is always difficult. It is the more shades – the ghosts of the dead days – that are dearest to me.

Spent my last day at school. De Quincey says (or was it Johnson?) that whenever we do anything for the last time, provided we have done it regularly for years before, we are a little melancholy, even though it has been distasteful to us . . . True.

Conrad Aiken 1889–1973

Number 58

aged 14

'Number 58? Duquesne Limited west-bound?' 'Yes, sir! track 27.
Leaves at 3:50. Through Pullman rear car but one. You'd better
hurry.'

It was a gray, stormy Christmas eve. I was going west to spend the
holidays with an aunt. I walked up to a line of shining Pullmans, and
scrambled aboard my car, just as a slow, heavy puff from the distant
engine sounded, and we gently pulled out of the station and plunged
into the tunnel ahead.

Upon leaving the tunnel our train was speeding through a dismal,
barren country. Brown, wind-swept field lay on either hand.
Deserted looking farmhouses clustered together at infrequent intervals. The north wind drove a torrent of cold rain against my window.
It was almost dusk, and, in the indistinct gloom, the landscape was so
dreary and deserted, that I turned away from my window, and began
to read the *Christmas Carol*, which I had brought with me.

Fifteen miles out, as ill luck would have it, we were flagged at a little
logging station, and, thanks to a freight accident, held two hours. As
we started up again at 6:15, it was with an unaccountable feeling of
discontent that I ate and settled myself for the evening with my book.
Everyone about me seemed jolly and full of Christmas cheer, but I
alone, companionless, huddled closer in my seat.

The conductor passed through the train, and I overheard him
talking with a jolly, red-cheeked, old gentleman, who was travelling
with a pretty, delicate, little girl.

'Yes, sir! everything's running behind time on this division just
now, I guess. Heavy traffic at this season. Oh, yes! I shouldn't wonder
if we made it up by morning. Just put on old 97 back at Pine Crag and
she'll bust her boiler to get us in on time. Well, I must be going
forward. A Merry Christmas to you!'

We certainly did seem to be going pretty fast. The train had now left the level country, and was thundering in and out among the mountain gorges; now rattling down grades, until the cars rocked, and creeked, and pitched, and swayed, and shivered, until it seemed as if they must leave the rails, then straining on the upgrades, while the engine puffed, and snorted, and tugged with a force greater than all the army of mighty Xerxes, pulling together, could have exerted. The rain had changed to hail and sleet, which, beating continuously against the window pane, accompanied, as it were, in dreary monotone the roaring of the wind and steam outside. As we climbed even higher into the northern uplands, even this ceased, and, by ten o'clock, gazing out of the window, I could see ghostly canyons and ridges gleaming in the moonlight.

As we were due in Saxonville before six the next morning, I went to bed without undressing. At length, lulled by the rumbling of the wheels, I fell asleep. Suddenly I felt a gust of cold air breathe upon me. I opened my eyes, and I was lying in the snow on a lonely mountain ridge. On one hand was a precipice within two feet of me, on the other a railroad track. As I raised myself, I heard the faint whistle of a locomotive far down in the valley, so hollow, even in the distance, that it made my blood run cold. I peered over the edge, and there, in the depths below me, threading its way over silvery loops of track, higher and ever higher, came a train. What particularly struck me about this train was that it was white, and I fancied I could see the track beneath it. Slowly it climbed upward, with many a twist and many a curve, until at length I saw it upon a moonlit mountain side, dashing straight towards me, seventy-five miles an hour. Not a light twinkled in the windows, and only a pale, ghastly, phosphorescent glow shone from the headlight. On it came, and, when but a thousand feet away, it whistled again, a loud, wild shriek, and my blood froze at the sound; but as it whistled, I heard a rush of air behind me, and, as I gazed, I saw a heavy freight train, dashing at the limited,[1] borne on by two mammoth engines at a tremendous speed. They struck about forty feet from me. With a rush of escaping steam, the engine of the limited leapt over the tearing, tottering cars in front of it, and made straight for me. As its shadowy form approached, I recoiled to the very edge of the rock wall, and, as it passed through me, albeit I could feel nothing,

---

[1] limited = an express.

I was seized with a chill so damp, so indescribably dreadful, that I cried out, as one who awakes from a nightmare. Then the engine leaped over the precipice, and, in an instant, struck upon the rocks a thousand feet below.

As I heard the crash, everything became real instead of phantom. Dim masses, hitherto spectral and shadowy, now showed forth clear and black against the moonlit snow. Here a pile of sturdy oaken beams were lying, splintered into kindling wood; there two dark monsters, hissing in their dying agonies, lay on their sides. Groans, sighs, pitiful cries, heartrending moans rose in the still night air all about me. By my side our brakeman, a big, stalwart young fellow, was lying, and the snow was crimson with his blood. Not far away lay the jolly cheeked old gentleman, the little girl clasped in his arms. I could not bear the sight, and, as my eyes grew dim, I sank back upon a body, already cold in the snow it lay upon.

When I came to, I was lying in a white bed, I knew not where. A nurse was bending over me, and, as I raised my head, a doctor came in. I was found to be uninjured, but badly shaken up. I listened with horrified ears as they told me of the awful disaster of the night before: how the Duquesne Limited, making up time, had struck a freight, running on cross orders, high up in the Black Indian range, and how but seven had been uninjured, of whom I was so fortunate as to be one. Thus, in thankfulness for my escape, I passed my Christmas, while the snows drifted outside over the little village and the lonely mountains, covering the wreckage and the bodies of those who had not been found.

Lex Talionis

aged 14

The wild beasts' law is the law of might,
    And the law of might is Death;
From the rising sun and the pall of night
    Till the dawning day's first breath,
The wild beast kills, till in turn he is killed –
    For the law of the beasts is Death.

At the age of twelve Conrad Aiken was disturbed when he discovered the law of the jungle – 'I mean that lions killed antelopes only themselves to be killed by man.' He wrote these lines:

The lions had waited all the day
Lying concealed in the grass for their prey . . .

When his father saw these lines he typed them out and gave them the title *Lex Talionis*. Two years later Aiken recast them in a different form, but preserved his father's title.

David Jones used to say that he was a painter before he was a poet, simply because the painting came before the poetry. He was seven years old when he made these pencil drawings of a 'Lion' and a 'Dancing Bear'. For the bear he borrowed his sister's ruler to put in the wooden fencing at the back. But she ticked him off roundly: 'No proper artist ever uses a ruler.'

Christopher Dawson 1889–1970

The Golden City and the Coal City

aged 6

CHAPTER I

Once upon a time there lived an emperor of 'The Golden City' he was going on a pilgrimage to win a city and have it for his own, and rule over it. This emperor was a saint and he was going to fight against a heathen city, and it was on the hill of nastiness, he was going to bring all his soldiers to fight against it, and he set off in the morning, and went to the beginning of a forest called the forest of warness and when he entered into it the bushes rustled and out sprang a dragon. When he saw this he ordered all his men to prepare for battle. The dragon on hearing this went to a palace of paper and went into it and the host followed it. When it got inside there was thousands of people it had took prisoner, but it thought to itself I cannot fight against this host or I shall get killed so I better try to do it, and the host on hearing this broke open all the chains, and let them loose, then they burnt up all the palace and out rushed the monster and fought. They burnt the animal soon and went on their way.

CHAPTER II

Soon they came near to a great army, from the coal city, and they said, will you give in – No! said they we won't give up. Then fight said the coal army, (they were heathens) and these Christians said they would fight, so the battle began. The heathens did shoot arrows of coal, and the soldiers of the golden city shot arrows of silver and gold. Soon a dragon plunged out of the forest and joined in the battle on the coal army's side. The golden city army won and went on their way.

Soon they got out of the forest and found they were on the bottom of the mountains of difficulty. Then they went up them and went to a palace that the prince of the City Beautiful lived in, and he asked them in to rest. Soon the Emperor asked him who he was king over, he said, your land, but what city is it? Why it is the City Beautiful that I am prince over said the prince. Well now we must go so goodbye. Where are you going to? asked the prince.

We are going to conquer the Coal City that is called by the name of Hateful City, for it is so wicked. It is true – we must be off – goodbye.

The Hateful City was on one of these hills, so they got to it, when the people of it heard this, they armed themselves and called all the people to the emperor of the Coal City. . . .

Sylvia Townsend Warner 1893–1978

Upon the Quality Called 'Romance'

aged 15

It is difficult to define Romance; it is like attempting to describe the air, it is so universal, so all-embracing. In everything done alone, and out-of-doors, there is much Romance. It lies in walking alone over the broad curving moors, in the tracking of a stream, in the discovery of some narrow rocky hollow, hidden away in the cleft of the hills: in a lesser degree, in the opening of a new book. Romance comes upon one suddenly in the friendly buffeting of the North Wind, in the tinkle of flowing water heard far off, in the sailing of a cloud's shadow down the opposite slope, across the valley between, and up the hillside to where one stands watching.

Walking alone on a winding road, what pageant may not come to one's sight, round the next bend, suddenly, with the abruptness of a kingfisher's flight over a clear pool; what challenge of dimly-heard music, borne on the freakish wind? The white gleam of the bent grass is really the sun-glitter on the lances of the armies, marching down into Roncesvalles; in that dark wood lies Medoro, and Angelica comes riding on her white palfrey looking for him; over that hillside, which is the Glistening Heath, rides Siegfried, girt with Gram, and wise with a new wisdom; as for that hawk circling high above me, it is really the wide-winged Hippogrif bearing Astolfo to the moon; and so all the well-known things of the moorland are changed by the subtle alchemy of Romance, as when a dark river-pool is lit by the shoaling bravery of the sun's rays, breaking of a sudden through a cloud.

The idea that runs through all Romance is the quest. It is the gold thread showing through the motley embroideries that the centuries have worked, and left unfinished; it is the search for guessed-at, unknown lands, for strange new beauty, for an ultimate good. It shows so strongly in the story of the Argonauts, the adventuring through strange lands, for a strange prize; in the Norse Sagas it reappears. Later, it becomes the search for the Sangreal; it comes again in the discovery of the New World, instinct with the strange possibilities of the unknown. Thus, shining with the same light amidst so many different surroundings, reflecting them, seemingly altered, yet still the same, as a stream born in the mountains flows down through placid pastures to the sea; thus goes this leit-motif of the quest, that can be traced in all true Romance.

There is a book which contains, for me, all the glamour of Romance, all the simplicity, all the idea of the quest: it is the *Pilgrim's Progress*. What more romantic than Christian's start? There is no material taking thought for the morrow; it has all the enthusiasm of the First Crusade: it is as if a child had said, 'I want to go along that road, and see where it leads to; there will be an enchanted castle at the end, I am sure, waiting for me; let's start,' whereupon he promptly starts. The main idea is simple, thereby becoming so romantic – the quest, the struggle for eternal beauty, the perilous journey through dark woods to the sunny green fields beyond.

Romance is one of the few things that all hold alike; every child is born with Romance inbred in it; it may be called by different names, it may even be made a term of opprobrium, but it is still as beautiful and as widespread as the red poppy; cultivation may strive to stamp it out, even as red poppies are combated; custom may change its guise, and impose restrictions upon it; but to what end? Romance is eternal, eternal as youth.

Robert Graves 1895–1985

The Dying Knight and the Fauns

aged 14

Through the dreams of yesternight
My blood-brother, great in fight,
I saw lying, slowly dying,
Where the weary woods were sighing
With the rustle of the birches,
With the quiver of the larches . . .
Woodland fauns with hairy haunches
Grin in wonder through the branches,
Woodland fauns that know no fear.
Wondering, they wander near,
Munching mushrooms red as coral,
Bunches too of rue and sorrel;
Wonder at his radiant fairness
At his dinted, shattered harness,
With uncouth and bestial sounds,
Knowing nought of war or wounds.
But the crimson life-blood oozes
And makes roses of the daisies,
Regal carpets of the mosses –
Softly now his spirit passes,
As the bee forsakes the lily,
As the berry leaves the holly;
But the fauns still think him living,
And with bay-leaves they are weaving
Crowns to deck him. Well they may!
He was worthy of the Bay.

The Miser of Shenham Heath

aged 15

A miser lived on Shenham Heath,
As lean and grey he was as Death;
All children feared his long grey beard,
His toes peeped from his boots uneath.[1]

Within the thatch he kept his store:
A thousand pounds of gold and more;
And every night, by candle-light,
Would take and count them o'er and o'er.

It chanced one chill November night,
He told the tale by candle-light,
When sudden fled from heart and head,
The lust for guineas round and bright.

Then, though that he was weak and old,
And though the waters glimmered cold,
A plunge he took in Shenham brook
And washed away the taint of gold.

He cast his clouts and donned instead
A suit he'd worn when he was wed;
The cloth was new, of red and blue;
A feathered hat adorned his head.

He rose at dawning of the day,
That none might meet him on his way;
To Chert he went and money spent,
But was not minded there to stay.

He bade a barber shave his chin,
And rode a-horse to Shenham Inn
In proper pride. The neighbours cried
"Soothly a lord, but ghastly thin."

From that day forth he would not cease
To feed the countryside like geese:
He lavished gold on young and old,
Till he had spent his last gold piece.

A pauper lives on Shenham Heath,
As lean and grey he is as Death;
All people fear to view him near,
His toes peep from his boots uneath.[1]

Merlin and the Child

aged 16

Merlin went up the mountain side.
A young boy stood above him and cried:
'Merlin, Merlin, where are you bound
Early, so early, with your black hound?
Your rod of hazel, well shaped and thin,
Do magic powers lie closed within?'

Merlin put two hands to his head,
Hiding his eyes in a terror, said:
'Lamb of thunder, avenging dove,
Dealer of wrath, High-king of love,
To search the way and the ways I am come
For a round red egg to carry home,
Blood-red egg of an ocean snake
From the hollowed stone where bright waves break,
To search if ever the valleys hold
Green watercress, or grass of gold,
By a woodland fountain-side to lop
The highest cluster from oak-tree top.
My hazel twig is a magic wand –
Magic of earth, and a power beyond.'

[1] Uneasily.

114

Close to Merlin the young boy stood,
Stretched his hand to the slender wood:
'Merlin, Merlin, turn now again!
Unharmed let the cluster of oak remain,
The cress in the valley where fresh brooks run,
The gold grass dancing below the sun,
And the smooth egg of your ocean snake
In the hollow where dappled waters shake.
Turn again in the steps you have trod:
There is no diviner, but only God!'

With regard to 'The Dying Knight and the Fauns', Robert Graves wrote to me on 4 December 1958: 'Mark the use of half-rhymes – e.g. "roses/daisies" and "mosses/passes" etc.' 'Merlin and the Child' he adapted from an early Cornish poem.

Ruth Pitter 1897–

Field grasses

aged 13

Purple and brown are they,
Purple and brown,
Yellow and silver-grey,
Clothing the down.
Dancing and nodding wise,
Gravely they go:
Bow to the wide blue skies,
Stately and slow.
Purple and brown are they,
Purple and brown,
All little ladies gay,
Treading the down.

Antonia White 1899–1979

The Copper Beech

aged 8

The Copper Beech is a native of England, and grows extremely well there.

GENERAL DESCRIPTION

The trunk is smooth and not very thick; the leaves are a dark reddish colour, and the branches, slender, wavy, and graceful. The bark is often of a silvery hue. The branches, if allowed to grow, sweep the ground. It looks best planted among other trees, whose leaves are green.

PARTS IN DETAIL

The trunk, as has been said, is smooth, and the bark a silvery grey – it does not peel off in patches like the Plane for instance. Sometimes the branches sweep the ground on one side, while on the other, they grow quite high up. This is because there are either trees on the side on which the branches are higher up, or that animals have eaten it.

In most cases it is the former. The buds are protected by scales, beautifully and ingeniously folded over the young leaf. The buds are long and thin. When the young leaves come out, they are folded like fans, and they gradually open out. They are also covered with tiny, silky hairs, to protect them from insects etc. They are a very deep red when they first come out, but after a time they get browner as they get older, and in late Autumn, they turn almost green. They grow alternately on the twig, and have net veins, also alternate. The smaller net veins are scarcely visible. The margin is wavy, and the leaf ends in a point. The inner leaves are usually greener than the (inner) more exposed ones, as the sun reaches the outer ones, but not the inner ones.

The fruit is the Beech nut, which is greatly liked by squirrels, it splits open the covering or 'mast', as it is called, and falls to the ground. The Clausilia Laminata[1] snails, which are very fond of Beech trees, are peculiarly like the bud-scales, when opened out.

THE BEECH TREE'S STORY

At one time, there were no Copper Beeches, for their leaves were green, like ordinary beeches; but how their leaves came to be red and therefore the tree was called Copper Beech, is here told.

It was May, the trees were all green, the sun was shining, and everyone and everything seemed to be happy, for the Summer was just coming. A soft breeze was sighing through a lovely wood, and in Nature language it said to the trees 'There will be a grand council to-night, be ready.' The trees waved their branches, which meant 'Yes, yes.'

About midnight, the wind gave a long whistle, which meant that the trees were to open their leaves, and attend this important council. A handsome horse-chestnut announced why this debate was to be held. 'Trees and saplings,' he began, 'We are about to decide who is to be our King, for the old oak, our great monarch, has fallen.' A suppressed whisper ran through the leaves of every tree. 'Each tree shall give its vote. Who votes for the young Oak?' A few did so. 'And who for the Elm?' 'O, he's too rugged,' chorused four or five.

Several others were mentioned but with very little success. The beech, who was very quiet and polite said 'I vote for the young oak, as our rightful King, and descendant of the old oak.'

No one took any notice of him, however. 'Who votes for the birch?' cried the tall horse-chestnut. 'I do' cried some but the elm said 'He's too slender and gets too agitated when the wind blows.'

The discussion went on, till the wind, passing, asked what the noise was about. They told him, and then he said 'Why don't you ask Mother Earth? She knows best.' The trees took his advice and despatched their messenger, the squirrel, to ask the great mother. Presently, there was a low rumbling, the earth was going to speak. 'I will give you a sign to-morrow, who shall be King, now sleep, O trees.'

Next morning, there was great excitement in the forest, as to who should wake-up first. The plane did so and saw to her surprise, that the

[1]A footnote to her father for whom the piece was written has been added in the margin: 'Can you give me any informat. on this?'

beech had turned a lovely dark red. The others soon awoke, and proclaimed the beech as the lawful King. The beech bowed politely his branches in the morning breeze, in answer to the compliments of his new subjects, and all the forest was happy.

Soon, the rumbling of Mother Earth was heard again, and this time she said 'All your saplings shall retain the royal red as their colour, O Copper Beech, for so I christen you. The other beeches will remain green, but yours will be the royal family, the Kings of the forest.'

The trees rustled loudly in applause and touched branches with each other and with the new King, in token of their good will and joy, and the sun poured down his beams smilingly on the happy forest, and the early birds sang a joyous carol of welcome to the new reign.

This is how the leaves became red, and the Copper Beech got its name.

Richard Hughes 1900–1976

Explanation, on Coming Home Late

aged 7

We went down to the river's brink
To of those clear waters drink,
Where the fishes, gold and red,
Ever quickly past us sped.

And the pebbles, red and blue,
Which we saw the green weeds through
At the bottom shining lay:
It was their shining made us stay.

Roy Campbell 1901–1957

Now, like a Ghost in Shadow Lands . . .

aged 14

Now, like a ghost in shadow lands,
The lamp-light fades away:
My fumbled pen, in weary hands,
Hath written all it may.

And yet remains superb, unsung,
A thought which is not mine,
A song to tuneless numbers rung,
Half human, half divine!

A second pausing, dream-beguiled,
I heard it swell and sway:
Till unattainable and wild
The echoes died away . . .

The morning woods are slumbering,
And drenched in silver dew:
Ah! that the song I could not sing
Might stir my breast anew.

The poem confirms Campbell's early habit, which lasted a lifetime, of writing at night.

Stevie Smith 1902–1971

Spanky-Wanky

aged 9

Spanky-Wanky had a sister
He said, I'm sure a black man kissed her
For she's got a spot just here
('Twas a beauty spot, my dear)
And it looks most awfully quaint
Like a spot of jet black paint.
But when he told his sister that
She threw at him her gorgeous hat
And with the airs that made her swanky
Said, I hate you Spanky-Wanky.

In August 1970 Stevie Smith rang to say: 'I'm sending you four items of juvenilia for your book.' Two, in fact, which she claimed were written in her teens, were not written until her twenties. Also one that she claimed to have written when she was nine years old was a spoof. 'I had hoped to catch you out,' she admitted later. Here, for the record, is the spoof:

Fairy Story
I went into the wood one day
And then I walked and lost my way
When it was so dark I could not see
A little creature came to me
He said if I would sing a song
The time would not be very long
But I must let him hold my hand tight
Or else the wood would give me a fright
I sang the song and then he let me go
But now I am home again there is nobody I know

Edward Upward 1903–

Gloom

aged 16

All in the silent, Autumn days,
   As I roamed bitterly,
It was still Gloom of leaf-starred ways
   Came following me.

It was still emerald Gloom of trees,
   All calm and mildly glad,
Came whispering great memories
   And dreams most sad.

And I loved Gloom, and dreamt with him,
   And loved the tales he had:
Oh! and I've happiness with him,
   For we are sad.

George Orwell 1903–1950

Awake! Young Men of England

aged 11

Oh! give me the strength of the Lion
  The wisdom of Reynard the Fox
And then I'll hurl troops at the Germans
  And give them the hardest of knocks.

Oh! think of the War lord's mailed fist,
  That is striking at England today:
And think of the lives that our soldiers
  Are fearlessly throwing away.

Awake! oh you young men of England,
  For if when your country's in need,
You do not enlist by the thousand
  You are truly cowards indeed.

Kitchener

aged 12

No stone is set to mark his nation's loss
   No stately tomb enshrines his noble breast;
Not e'en the tribute of a wooden cross
      Can mark his hero's rest.

He needs them not, his name untarnished stands,
   Remindful of the mighty deeds he worked,
Footprints of one, upon time's changeful sands,
      Who ne'er his duty shirked.

Who follows in his steps no danger shuns,
   Nor stoops to conquer by a shameful deed,
An honest and unselfish race he runs,
      From fear and malice freed.

William Plomer 1903–1973

Epigram: to a Profane but Entertaining
Companion in a Tent

aged 16

Pray hang the night with wordy tapestries:
And every time you swear, that word
Among the leaves of talk shall seem a bird.

Christopher Isherwood 1904–1986

Mapperley Plains

aged 16

By the swift ways of shade and sun
We trod the morning. Spring was white
And hushed in lovely pools of light –
But we were eager to have won
Mapperley Plains, so strange and fair;
Nor guessed what should await us there.

And strong noon bridged half Heaven in flame
And day swung down from blue to blue . . .
We marched untired, for we knew
Daylight could never be the same,
Or Glory half so glad, as when
The weird plains seize the hearts of men.

Their beauty is the sword that cleaves
Youth, royally lived in pride and laughter,
From blank, prosaic Age. Hereafter
A bright day's ending . . . fallen leaves –
Mapperley Plains are years behind,
Their music dies within the mind.

The poem was written one late afternoon, after getting back from an Officers'
Training Corps field-day. The name 'Mapperley Plains' had thrilled Isherwood as a
boy, as he repeated it again and again to himself. Only years later did he learn that it
was a residential suburb of Nottingham.

Evelyn Waugh 1903–1966

The Curse of the Horse Race

aged 7

CHAP I   BETTING

'I bet you 500 pounds I'll win.' The speaker was Rupert, a man of about 25, he had a dark bushy mistarsh and flashing eyes.

'I should not trust to much on your horse' said Tom for ineed he had not the sum to spear.

The race was to take place at ten the following morning.

CHAP II   THE RACE

The next morning Tom took his seat in the grant stand, while Rupert mounted Sally (which was his horse) with the others to wate for the pistol shot which would announse the start.

The race was soon over and Rupert had lost. What was he to do, could he do the deed? Yes I'll *kill* him in the night, he thought.

CHAP III   THE FIRE

Rupert crept stedfustly along with out a sound but as he drew his sword it squeeked a little. This awoke Tom. Seasing a candle he lit it just at that moment Rupert struck – and sent the candle flying. The candle lit the curtain.

Rupert trying to get away tumbled over the bed. Tom maid a dash for the door and clided[1] with a perlisman who had come to see what was the matter and a panic took place.

CHAP IIII   EXPLAIND

While Tom and the peliesman were escapeing through the door, Rupert was adoping quite a diffrant methard of escape. He puld the

[1]clided = collided.

matris off the bed and hurled it out of the window, then jumped out. He landed safe and sound on the matris, then began to run for all he was worth. Now let us leave Rupert and turn to Tom and the peliesman. As soon as they got out Tom told the peliesman what had hapend.

CHAP V HOT ON THE TRAIL

'See there he is' said Tom. 'We must follow him and take him to prizen' said the peliesman.

'Theres no time to spere' said Tom. 'Letts get horses' said the peliesman, so they bort horses and [went] galerpin in the direction they had seen him go.

On they went until they were face to face with each other. The peliesman lept from his horse only to be stabed to the hart by Rupert. Then Tom jumped down and got Rupert a smart blow on the cheak.

CHAP VI A DEADLY FIGHT

This enraged Rupert that he shouted and made a plung, but Tom was too quick for him artfully dogeing[1] the sword. He brout his sword round on Rupert's other cheak.

---

[1]dogeing = dodging.

Just at that moment Rupert slashed [and] killed the peliesmans horse, then lept on Toms horse and galapt off.

CHAP VII   THE MYSTERIOUS MAN

Of course there was no chance of catching him on foot so Tom walked to the nearest inn to stay the night, but [as] it was full up he had to share with another man.

Though Tom was verry tired, he could not sleep. Their was something about the man . . . he did not like. He reminded him of some one [but] he did not know who. Suddenly he felt something moveing on the bed. Looking up he saw the man fully dressed, just getting off the bed.

CHAP VIII   RUN TO ERTH

Now Tom could see that the mysterious man was Rupert. Has he come to do a merder? Or has he only come to stay the night? These were the thoughts that rushed throu Toms head.

He lay quite still to [see] what Rupert would do first. He opend a cubord and took out a small lether bag from this, he took some thing wich made Toms blud turn cold. It was a pistol. Tom lept forward and seased Rupert by the throught[1] and flung him to the ground. Then snaching a bit of rope from the ground he bound Rupert hand and foot.

CHAP IX   HUNG

Then Tom drest himself, then Tom took Rupert to the puliese and Rupert was hung for killing the peliesman. I hope this story will be a leson to you never to bet.

---

[1]throught = throat.

Referring to this story in June 1960, during a television interview with John Freeman, the author said: 'Betting was not a temptation to which my father was at all subject, since he was never at a race-course in his life.' But Waugh had had a Calvinist nanny who had warned him against the dangers of gambling.

Multa Pecunia

aged 9

CHAPTER I

Sir Alfred James, a great collector of books, one day chanced to look at
an old volume which had the curious name of 'MULTA PECUNIA',
which told him that under his house there was a cave in which was
untold of wealth. He did not trouble to read any more, for he had
heard the yarn before, and did not believe it.

When Tom came home, being Sir Alfred's son, he was treated with
great respect by the servants and therefore was allowed to go into
every nook and corner of the house. He was in a little poky room one
day, when he saw this carving 'MULTA PECUNIA'. He stared for some
time at the carving, when suddenly he remembered seeing a book in
the library with the same title. Immediately he ran to the library and
took out the catalogue. There he saw these words, 'MULTA PECUNIA,
SHELF 7, PLACE 13'. He was immediately at shelf 7, but place 13 was
empty!

CHAPTER II

What could it mean? Why had the book gone? He was quite
bewildered. 'Jumping Golliwogs' cried Tom at last, 'I must tell the
Pater.' He left the room with the intention of going to tell his father
about the mysterious disappearance of the old volume; perhaps his
father had it, or – Hark! what was that? The rustling of stiff paper was
audible. He was now quite close to Smith [in] the butler's room. The
door was open so he looked in. There he saw Smith leaning over the
old volume deeply engrossed. Suddenly he got up and walked
stealthily to the door. Then he walked off in the direction of the room
with the carving. When he got there he pressed the letter 'U' and
immediately a little trap door opened which was about 17 by 13
inches. Into this crept Smith followed by Tom. The two crept along a
passage, and stopped at the sight of a great granite door. 'Smith! what
does this mean?' cried Tom putting his hand on Smith's collar. Smith
fairly staggered when he saw Tom; in fact he simply lost his head, and
flew at Tom's throat. A tremendous fight ensued in which Tom with
his knowledge of boxing gave him, gave Smith an 'up shot' blow that

fairly staggered him. But in the end weight won and Tom was knocked senseless to the ground: but Smith was not a fellow to leave him there, he carried him up the steps and laying him down at the door of the library, then closing the door of the secret cave, and putting back the old volume in the library as he found it, he went back to bed.

Sir Alfred came striding along the passage to the library when he suddenly stopped in utter astonishment. 'Tom!' he gasped as he saw the boy's pale face.

CHAPTER III

When Tom came to consciousness he found himself in a soft feather bed with a nurse at his bedside. 'Ah! that's good, he is conscious now' she whispered. 'Why did Smith attack me?' asked Tom feebly. 'He's delirious' said the nurse turning to the doctor, 'I thought he would be after that fall, poor boy'. For the library being at the foot of a flight of steps, Sir Alfred and the nurse naturally thought he had fallen down them.

A long time had past and Tom had not been allowed to see anyone as he had concussion of the brain. At last he was allowed to see someone and nurse asked him who he would choose for his first visitor. 'Smith' was the reply. In came Smith very shyly. 'Why did you fling me down on that stone' demanded Tom.

CHAPTER IV

Now Smith was not usually a butler. He was really a proffesional thief and so he soon thought of what to say, so turning to the nurse he said 'I think I had better go for the excitement of seeing anybody after such a long time of quiet has made him a bit mad'. With that he left the room.

Tom was quite well and able to run about the house, so he thought he would see Smith. Smith was not in his room, so Tom thought that he would go into the secret cave. He went to the old carving, pressed the letter 'U', immediately the same door opened. He went along the passage. Suddenly he stopped abruptly, for footsteps could be heard coming towards him. He crouched down waiting ready to spring. The footsteps came nearer and nearer. Tom could feel his heart thumping against his ribs. Suddenly [Smith] appeared round the corner of the passage, Tom was on him in a minute and, taken by surprise, Smith was flung senseless to the ground. Tom was just

getting up when he saw a piece of old parchment, he opened it and this is what he read – 'I, Wilfred James have stolen these articles of great price from Queen Elizabeth. I could not keep the secret so I put my confidence in Sir Walter Raleigh who gave a hint about it to the great statesman Bacon, who told Queen Elizabeth. The troops of soldiers will be here in one hour and if they find the jewels I shall be locked in the Tower.' There the paper ended, so Tom began to look for the jewels, and found them in Smith's pocket. Then putting Smith back on his bed, he went to his father's study and told Sir Alfred all the paper had said, and showed him the jewels.

The next day Sir Alfred gave Smith the 'sack' and the day after he was found to be the worst thief that ever puzzled Scotland Yard and was arrested and sent to Dartmoor convict prison.

Graham Greene 1904–

Confessions

aged 7

What is your greatest aim in life?	To go up in an aeroplane.
What is your idea of happiness?	Going up to London.
Who is the greatest living statesman?	Don't know any.
Who is your favourite character in fiction?	Dixon Brett.[1]
What are the qualities you admire most in men?	Good looks.
What are the qualities you admire most in women?	Cleanliness.
What is your favourite pastime?	Playing Red Indians.
What is your pet hobby?	Collecting coins.
What is your favourite quotation?	'I with two more to help me will hold the foe in play.'[2]
Which is the author you like best and which book?	Scott: *The Talisman.*
Who is the cricketer you most admire?	Herbert Greene.[3]
Which is your favourite holiday resort?	Overstrand.

[1]A detective.
[2]From Macaulay: *Lays of Ancient Rome, Horatius,* stanza XXIX.
[3]Eldest brother.

Henry Green 1905–1973

Sermon

aged 8

Brethren you know the time Jesus told Peter that he would deny him
thrice and then the cock would crow and I expect you remember how
Peter did deny that he had been with Jesus and how after three times
denying of having been with Jesus the cock crew and how he went out
and wept. Now Brethren to be frank I think that it did Peter a great
deal of good for he was a very weak man. I think it hardened him for
sorrow, some great sorrow generally hardens a person's heart and
prepares him for more bad things to come, it hardened him for the
long endurance of preaching to all the heathen races and baptising
them. But he was not altogether cured for when they searched to
crucify him he ran away and as he was travelling a road he saw a vision
of Jesus, and Peter asked Jesus what he was going to do. Jesus said: 'I
am going to be crucified for you' and Peter stopped Jesus and said he
would go. Brethren, I think that shows that Peter was still rather weak
not that I should not run away for probably I should though I must
admit it needs a very strong mental brain to stop in a town where you
knew you were going to be crucified in about a week's time but still it
does show a weakness in faith and in mental power. Now let us turn to
Jesus, who had come down in order to be crucified for Peter, what
power of mental brain he had. Now Brethren let me describe the cross
as the right path for Peter to take otherwise the thing he knew was
right to do and the devil on the other side showing what pains he
would have to bear and how nice it would be to run away out of the
town and preach in another, so he had a veritable battle between good
and evil but alas Brethren evil got the better of him and he ran away.
Then Our Lord came and offered to be crucified for him showing his
wonderful love for Peter not only for Peter but for the whole world,
but Peter could not bear to see his Lord be crucified so he went back
saying he was not fit to be crucified head up so he was crucified head

downwards. Now Brethren always try and do what Peter did after he saw Our Lord going to be crucified for him and conquer evil not that any one of us will be but I mean conquer your evil thoughts and always try to do what you know is right.

Henry Green wrote to me on 21 November 1958: 'I have three sermons . . . written at the age of 8 which I strongly recommend.' This, it seems, is the only surviving one – though when he included it in his autobiography *Pack my Bag* (1942) he claims that he was twelve when he composed it.

John Betjeman 1906–1984

The Snow

aged 8

Calm and silent be the weather,
But the wind, is keen and cold.
Let snow cover moor's of heather
Let it cover turf and mould.
  It falls so sweetly,
  And lands so neatly,
Upon the dirty ground
  So sweet and light,
  So powdery white
Like wool around.
Calm and silent be the weather,
But the wind, is keen and cold.
Let snow cover moor's of heather
Let it cover turf and mould.

THE SNOW

31 WEST HILL

HIGHGATE
N

BY J. Betjemann

Calm and silent be the weather,
But the wind, is keen and cold.
Let snow cover moors of heather
Let it cover turf and mould.
   It falls so sweetly,
     And lands so neatly,
Upon the dirty ground.
   So sweet and light,
     So powdery white
Like wool around
Calm and silent be the weather,
But the wind, is keen and cold.
Let snow cover moors of heather
Let it cover turf and mould.

            J. Betjemann

aged 8½.

Summer Poem

aged 13

Whatever will rhyme with the summer?
There only is 'plumber' and 'drummer':
Why! the cleverest bard
Would find it quite hard
To concoct with the Summer, – a plumber!

My mind's getting glummer and glummer.
Hooray! *there's* a word besides drummer;
Oh, I will *think* of some
Ere the prep's end has come,
But the rimes will get rummer and rummer.

Ah! – If the bee hums, it's a hummer;
And the bee showeth signs of the Summer;
Also holiday babels
Make th' porter gum labels,
And whenever he gums, he's a gummer!

The cuckoo's a goer and comer,
He goes in the hot days of Summer;
But he cucks ev'ry day
Till you plead and you pray
That his voice will get dumber and dumber!

Ode on a Mid-Victorian Centre Ornament

aged 16

Oh thou maid of buxom beauty!
   Lifting up to hold the cake
An impossible creation,
   Which is surely a mistake,
I have often wept in thinking
   How terribly your arms must ache.

Oh thou fish in beauty trailing
   At each corner, are you dead?
If you are not I will warn you
   'Lie the other way instead
Staying long in that position
   Makes the blood run to your head.'

Oh you thousand strange devices
   Can you tell me what you mean
By trailing creepy curly tendrils
   Over every varied scene
Infringing on the neat inscription
   'A presentation to the dean . . .'?

W. H. Auden 1907–1973

The Traction Engine

aged 16

Its days are over now; no farmyard airs
Will quiver hot above its chimney-stack; the fairs
It dragged from green to green are not what they have been
    In previous years.

Here now it lies, unsheltered, undesired,
Its engine rusted fast, its boiler mossed, unfired,
Companioned by a boot-heel and an old cart-wheel,
    In thistles attired.

Unfeeling, uncaring; imaginings
Mar not the future; no past sick memory clings,
Yet it seems well to deserve the love we reserve
    For animate things.

The Engine House

aged 16

It was quiet in there after the crushing
Mill; the only sounds were the clacking belt
And the steady throb of waters rushing
That told of the wild joy those waters felt
In falling. The quiet gave us room to talk:
'How many horse-power is the large turbine?'
'Seventy. The beck is dammed at Greenearth Fork:
Three hundred feet of head. The new pipe-line
Will give another hundred though, at least;
The mill wants power badly.' He turned a wheel;
The flapping of the driving-belt increased
And the hum grew shriller. He wiped a steel
Rail with a lump of waste. 'And now,' he said,
'I'll show you the slimes-house and the vanning shed –
This way.' He opened a small wooden door
And the machinery leaped into a roar.

These poems originally appeared in Christopher Isherwood's semi-fictional book
Lions and Shadows (1937) and were attributed there to 'Hugh Weston'.

Kathleen Raine 1908–

On an Autumn Evening

aged 12

1

Far in the west the great sun is
    sinking low
Upon a glowing couch of purple
    cloud;
And 'ere he sinks to sleep beneath
    night's shroud
He sheds upon the earth a
    lingering glow.

2

The blue smoke rises slow
    from woodland fires
The purple heather merges
    into sky,
The half dazed bees now feel the
    winter nigh
And each to honeychargéd
    hive retires.

3

The laden orchard boughs hang
    to the ground;
The gentle breezes through the
    tree tops sigh;
Grey layers of mist along the
    hollows lie,
And reedy brooks give forth
    a murmuring sound.

4

The wheeling swallows twitter
    in the air;
A thousand dewdrops sparkle
    on the ground;
And all the half bare
    hawthorn twigs are bound
With ropes of shimmering
    elfin diamonds rare.

5

The mellow light pours through
    the stainéd panes
Of peaceful churches, ivy clad
    and grey.
Now one by one departs each
    lingering ray
And solemn silence o'er all
    nature reigns.

Jocelyn Brooke 1908–1966

Surrey

aged 8

Surrey seems one of the great nature districts – as far as Camberley, Frimley, and other villages go. But as in all other counties the bustle of town life seems as if it cannot keep out. For instance, a man who has business at Guildford passing Frimley on his way, would perhaps even scorn anyone who would take the trouble to wade through rushes and purple loose-strife, for the sake of getting a root of branched bur-reed. No, legs are meant to carry you, even if the water is a foot deep. Does Camberley hold anything but nature, peace and pleasure?

CHAPTER I

Surrey is enough to drive a botanist wild. In one spot, near the Barossa golf-links, which is Crown Land, a rare species of mullion is to be found, near to it is what one might call a bed of Orpine, clashing with the white and blue of lupins. All these go into one final clash, with sheets of heather and rosebay. From here can be seen Turf Hill, with its flagstaff on the top, the sun's rays turned purple with all species of heath.

Amongst all this the small streets of Camberley nestle. In the grass small blue violas brighten the blank spaces. Towering above them stand hollyhocks and foxgloves. Among these beautiful peacocks, red admirals, brimstones and other rare butterflies flutter. On the bushes birds twitter and feast. With them flutter enormous meadow-browns, some sitting, with stretched-out proboscis, too full of honey to move. For blues and small coppers, large clumps of golden rod are to be had. It has seven petals, making quite a rest for the butterflies.

CHAPTER 2

Frimley is different to Camberley one way, this way is that it is a bog, or marsh. It is a mixture of purple loose-strife, rushes, branched bur-reed, yellow loose-strife, and all species of bog plants. The description seems to come easily in poetry, thus –

Where the purple loose-strife grows
Where the river runs and flows
With its upright purple spike
Which it bends towards the light.

This when first read seems as if it only describes purple loose-strife, but when read and understood it describes the whole of Frimley.

When Camberley is reached it is easy to get to Blackwater, and York Town. Certainly, these two towns (at least almost towns) do not hold anything interesting, but it is easier to get to Frimley if the traveller stops at Blackwater. If a list of plants was made, all that grew in Surrey, a quarter of it might go like this:–

Purple Loose-strife .... Frimley
Meadowsweet .... Frimley
Yellow Loose-strife .... Camberley
Branched Bur-reed .... Frimley
Common Heath .... Camberley
Ling .... Camberley
Marsh Thistle .... Frimley
Moth Mullion .... Camberley
Orpine .... Camberley

CHAPTER 3

To go back to the Barossa golf-links:

Along a country lane in summer
The golden rod, with lifted stem
Longing for the cooling rain
Soon begins to droop.
But when the rain comes pouring down
It lifts its head to reach the sun.

Now if there is one species of flower growing round Camberley, there are a thousand. Not to say that all the natural orders of England collect in Surrey, but all the southern species. And as to Lepidoptera, the Barossa golf-links are almost like the Aurora Borealis! And again,

Camberley is noted for the Royal Military College; to botanists, it should be more noted for flowers. I have often sat by a hedge at the Golf Links waiting with a net for butterflies, while the bees and other flies keep up a loud buzz.

CHAPTER 4

It is the truth a small thing often holds the best things. This is so with Surrey. No one could call it a big county, though it holds a few pretty large towns, such as Kingston, Croydon and Guildford. Otherwise, it is fairly overflowing with nature. It is true I have only been there a month but even a week is a long enough time to see Surrey is not a county for towns. The Camberley heath is a beautiful sight. Imagine a sea of purple fire with a few fir trees looming like the coral islands of the Pacific Ocean! Out of all the counties I have ever been to, Kent, Surrey, Sussex and Hants, it is fuller of nature than all.

Malcolm Lowry 1909–1957

Hockey Dramatics

aged 16

Leys v. Guys March 11th, 1926: Won, 2– 1

A question which is about on a par with such rhetorical taxes on the brain as 'Should we eat more Fruit?', 'What is wrong with France?' and 'Shall we sing hymn No. 403?' but which I have seen neither printed, published nor promulgated – nor, for that matter, have I heard it propounded – is 'Can there be any romance in Hockey?' or, let me put it this way, 'Should one introduce romance in reporting Hockey?' Admittedly there must be some in Rugby football, e.g. a reporter may remark that 'the Blackheath flier, having eluded his erstwhile club-mate, smacked the oval down between the uprights as calmly as if it had been a parallelopiped'; in Association he may chat glibly about moieties, custodians and referees whom he strongly advises to play the game in Port Sunlight, if it is not their custom in West Kirby; in Cricket he may say that the batsman 'smote the leather hurtling across the turf, flying figure after flying figure trying to impede the progress of the globular Juggernaut, but . . .' Now Hockey, though one of the few games common to both sexes, has, I take it, little romance in it; and the reporter, whether he is trying to argue for or against the merits of journalese, if he introduces any cheerful romancing into his report, has to be prepared for [the] prattlings of puerile pedants.

I am called upon to write a report of a match which, frankly, is not worth reporting. *Quid igitur faciam*? Hesitating to write a straight-forward report I can compare the thing, at any rate, to a poor play, about as good as – let me see now – Countess Cathcart's 'Ashes'. It is, I suppose, in two acts (unlike 'Ashes', which has three), the first act about as diverting as a musical comedy without any music; the second as a farce without a single laugh, without a single epigram; the play with two tame curtains (I stayed only for one), yet played in a theatre of excellent traditions and many previous successes. Rocyn-Jones, that famous actor, played a poor part; not only did he forget his lines more than once, but, sulkily, quite failed to respond to the voice of the prompter, and stood gagging helplessly to an audience, which, while it gave him no support, was curiously well-behaved. He must be held chiefly responsible for the fact that the play was not an overwhelming success. Taylor was suffering from stage fright, and missed several cues. He should, although I fear he will not, be tried again. Those excellent artistes, L. H. Birch, K. W. Birch, and N. E. Dainty, continued to be excellent, but what could they do at the back of the stage with such poor support in front? Masina, so promising, made the unforgiveable mistake of shuffling his feet while delivering his lines; E. R. Hargreaves and P. G. Nichol – good men both – were drawn down in the general depression. W. S. Green and J. M. Smith were as irreproachable as ever, but what could they do by themselves? It was slightly before the final curtain that I crept (complete with hump) towards a door which, had it been there, would have been surmounted tactfully with the legend EXIT.

A Rainy Night

aged 16

Somerset Maugham declares that the rain in tropical regions has a depressing and demoralising effect upon the inhabitants. It numbs the brain – this monotonous, almost deafening hiss – causing people to do things that otherwise they would never dream of doing. Never having been to the South Sea Isles, however, I can only take his word for it. Still, here in comparatively unromantic England I once committed a terrible, though I suppose, quite excusable blunder, while it was raining.

Heavens! how it rained!

My excuse for blundering is obvious; my excuse for writing this rather futile prologuette – if I may thus coin a word – is perhaps not so obvious. However . . .

It was in December. The morning had broken cold and bleak, and gave every promise of rain. I was not displeased at this, for I had a long railway journey before me – Yeovil to Liverpool, to be exact – (one has to run up to Manchester and down again to get there – rather silly), which normally is a very tiring and monotonous one.

However, when it is raining I confess to a sort of infantile pleasure in listening to the rain pattering outside. If it is fine on such occasions, I always feel that it is my luck to have to spend a day travelling when I might be on the golf links – in fact, every course of which it is possible to obtain a brief cinematographic view as we pass inspires me with a desire to take my clubs from the rack, jump out, and have a game. On wet days things are very different. The flags on the greens, which are full of troubled pools, are so soaked as to have lost most of their flapping power. The bunkers are full of water. The fairways are punctuated with miniature lakes, with green shoots of grass appearing above the surface, looking as though the whole casual water (pardon the homely simile) was a bald man's head boasting still a few treasured hairs on top. The only signs of life are perhaps one disconsolate and half-soaked greenkeeper sheltering (he is not fully soaked because he has been sheltering most of the morning), a sodden sheep or two, maybe . . .

All this, when you have arranged for a game, is one of the most depressing spectacles on God's earth. When you cannot play, the irony of circumstances may make it one of the most comforting.

The various towns and villages which we passed through just before we reached Manchester looked slightly more repelling than usual. Moreover, when we reached that town it was dark. Outside, the rain having decided not to be half-hearted about things, lashed down as though the ground were a ceiling which it must penetrate at all costs. Everywhere sodden advertisements clung like wet rags. I caught glimpses of mackintoshed mothers and sons drinking coffee in waiting rooms, more people outside with umbrellas, more advertisements . . .

But it was cosy in my third class compartment. I seemed to be about the only person on the train, and with the lights on, a good magazine for company, and the home-coming at Liverpool to look forward to, I could not have been more contented.

In the meantime the rain was fairly sweeping against the window.

My host in the south, being one of those almost too obliging fellows, had insisted on having some sandwiches made up for me for the journey. I did make a protest, as a matter of fact, but it was received in a 'No-no-my-dear-chap – no-trouble-whatever – no-trouble-whatever' sort of voice, so in the end I accepted his offer. But as they proved to be salmon, a fish which I abhor, I decided to have lunch on the train, and the sandwiches remained forgotten in my bag.

We were on the short run home to Liverpool.

With a feeling of boredom I threw down my magazine and edged myself into the corridor. I strolled up and down. The train appeared to be empty except for a little wizened, cross-eyed old man, who shivered in the corner of the corridor. I approached him.

'Why not come and sit down in the carriage? It must be rather cold out there,' I ventured.

'Aye not like sit in carriage in – these,' replied the man, indicating his clothing.

He spoke with a decided accent: what nation it belonged to I could not for the moment determine. He mumbled rather.

'Why, good lord, man,' I said, 'there's hardly another soul on the train. Anyhow, what if there were?'

'Py Jo! Aye forgat.' He spoke hurriedly. 'It's very kind of you.' He came and sat down in my compartment.

'Not a bit, the railway company supply the seats. The obvious thing to do, as far as I can see, is to sit in them – having paid your fare . . .'

'Ah! dat is it,' said he slowly, 'aye have not paid my fare. Your station-master – he pity me . . . Py Jo! Aye forgat.'

'You forgat what?' I queried before I had time to realise the rudeness of the echo. 'Tell me the whole story,' I added.

I regarded my companion acutely (why must we always regard our companions acutely, by the way?). His cross eyes were glazed and seemed almost to be standing out of his head. His skin was greasy, where skin could be seen for dirt.

'Drink!' I thought: 'That's it. He does seem a curious man, and not English by the looks of him. German perhaps?' No, he didn't seem to be German. I put his age down at about sixty.

As if in answer to my question: 'Aye vas Svedish – Olivsen my name,' he said. 'Fireman on board *Tasmania*. Sailed from Manchester last night. Aye pick it up at Liverpool tonight. Olivsen – square-head name. Oder name Christofersen – vorse!'

'A fireman's life is pretty strenuous, isn't it?' I asked. 'How did you come to miss your boat, by the way?'

'Aye vas ill,' he replied simply.

For a moment I thought he was going to faint, but he seemed to recover himself. I was almost on the point of giving him a lecture on the distressing consequences of liquor, but I pulled up in time.

'Of course,' I added, keeping up the conversation, 'most of the ships are driven by oil now, aren't they?'

'Yes. Py Jo,' he said. 'Aye forgat.' Then, quietly and rather indistinctly: 'My life has been one tragedy.'

'Aye gat news on my last voyage that my kiddie . . . he vas dead. Aye live in your country, you know. Aye hardly recover from news. Vhen I get back home, my vife – she had cleared.'

'Good lord!' I ejaculated, really sorry for the little fellow. 'Cleared? Do you mean she ran off with another man?'

'Vith oder man, no. Cleared – dead – like may kiddie. Py Jo!' he added brokenly. 'Aye hardly recover from news.'

'Oh!' I felt I couldn't say much else in the circumstances. Yet, though I hated myself for doing it, I almost added – 'and that's why you took to drink,' but I pulled myself up in time.

'Aye felt too ill to gat on boat last night,' he continued. 'She sail. Aye have no money to pick *Tasmania* up at Liverpool, where she spend the night. Aye vhalk to station and tell station-master may trouble. He have compassion and gat me ticket. That why I like not sit in compartment as you say.'

'Well, if that's all your trouble . . . Money . . .' I fingered my note-case.

'No,' he broke out, holding up his hand: 'No! my pride already injured enough. I not take money from oder man. Dat station-master he very good, but if Aye had not been ill – vould sooner have vhalked to Liverpool – Py Jo! Aye forgat.' And he rambled on – a prolific talker, I thought; and though I was ashamed of the thought, I felt that it was a good thing I hadn't given the money, for he would only have spent it on drink. Yet – he refused. Funny . . .

We were nearing the slums of Liverpool. A strong wind had risen. Through the blurred windows I could see a phantasmagoria of moving lights partly obscured by the driving rain which lashed up against the windows in sudden whipping gusts. The wind whined in the telegraph wires. Slums – dirt – houses, in drab blocks of the same dull design; but there were lights in some of the windows betokening at any rate some vitality. It was more than poor Olivsen had. He pointed out the sight with a stubby forefinger belonging to a hand greased and grimed with indelible grime.

'It is more than Aye haf,' he said sadly, speaking my thoughts. He stopped.

'Drink,' I began; but I couldn't think quite how to go on, so I changed the subject. But, all the same, I felt pretty certain of the kind of illness that had prevented him from catching this boat.

We were nearing Central station then, plunging through the maze of tunnels which occur just outside the city.

'Now look here,' I said, suddenly magnanimous in the spirit of the season, 'we're getting near Liverpool now. It's a perfect beast of a night; you simply can't go dashing around catching boats. Suppose you come with me and I'll give you a job as a gardener or something at my place. I need one, by the way. And here's a couple of –' I never finished the sentence, though I had started fingering my note-case again.

'Tank you, no!' he interrupted, holding up his hands. 'You are very kind. But I haf to do my duty by *Tasmania*. Aye sign on.'

'Good lord!' I began, 'they won't mind. Just –'

'Aye gat yob,' he continued. 'Aye hope keep yob. Aye take no money from anyone except for work Aye do. But you are very kind.'

'Well if you won't –' I said, rather surprised, replacing my note-case.

'Well, here's Central. Good-bye, old Swede.' And I stepped out into the corridor, threw open a window and engaged a porter almost in the same breath; and in the joy of seeing my wife, I forgot Olivsen entirely.

The latter still remained seated in the carriage. 'Old Svede!' he repeated to himself; 'that what he call me' (with a laugh). 'And Aye am only thirty-two!'

He half rose . . .

★ ★ ★

That night the man whose business it is to go round the empty carriages, tapping the wheels, collecting the railway corporation teacups and articles that have been left behind on the rack by the unwary, found a dead man in an empty compartment.

He called his mate, and the two of them carried the body into the waiting room. The first man rang for a doctor. In the meantime, though it was quite late, a considerable crowd had gathered round. Eventually the doctor arrived, accompanied by a policeman.

The latter reproved the workmen for moving the body. The doctor made his examination, making the startling discovery that the man, who bore letters upon his person addressed to Christofersen Olivsen, had died of starvation. The body was removed to the mortuary, and further investigations were postponed until the next day.

★　★　★

At about the same time my wife was unpacking my kit-bag, laughing at my usual untidiness.

'Hello!' she remarked, as she noticed a certain parcel, 'you're absent-minded as well as untidy, now, my man. Why, you've forgotten your lunch!'

William Sansom 1912–1976

Caught in his own Trap

aged 10

One night Mr Nicolas Fuster was sitting in a cab which was making its way carefully along the Strand. Then the Driver turned a corner sharply and climbed a small hill. After traversing many roads he came to a little alleyway and stopped. Mr Fuster climbed out and gave the driver some money and told him to wait. Mr Fuster, who we shall call 'Fuster', walked up the steps of a house called 'Carew Manor'. He knocked at the door, and, lighting a cigar, waited. A wizened old butler came to the door and said, 'Wat name, sir? Mr Nayland Smith is in 'is room sir, wait till I calls 'im sir.' Fuster answered in the affirmative, told his name and said that he would go to Nayland Smith's study, instead of that worthy troubling to come down. He passed into a well-furnished, but small, hall, and hung his hat and coat up and proceded up the stairs. He arrived at the landing and was motioned towards a small door. He knocked and entered. He found himself confronted by a tall thick set man with dark hair, blue eyes, ruddy complexion, thickset jaw and no moustache or beard. He was wearing a grey flannel suit & had crêpe rubber shoes. He motioned Fuster to a seat and questioned him as to his name, business and so on. Fuster then said, 'Nayland Smith, I am in great trouble. My butler, who served me faithfully for ten years, was taken upon from behind and was tyed up when he was taking care of the house for me; after drugging him they, the robbers or whatever they were, stole all the valuables and stuck a needle into Jenkin my butler's arm, sending him absolutely Mad. Its a great pity sir because I, being, or having been a millionaire, had a wonderful collection of jewels that cost five thousand pounds. They are all gone now sir, and I am afraid I shall have to sell the house. Its a pity, as I told you before Mr Smith, because that old house has been with my family for five centuries.' Nayland

Smith placed his fingertips together and said, 'I will help you as much as I can, Mr Fuster.' After that he said he would like Mr Fuster to stay the night and that he would accompany him to his house in the morning.

Nayland Smith and Fuster were in the train speeding along to Bromley House, the home of Fuster. Suddenly the train made a jolt and slowed down to a standstill. Nayland Smith found that they had arrived at their destination and he and Fuster descended from the carriage onto the platform. They produced their tickets and gave them to the collector and walked up to a horse and trap, which belonged to Fuster. They climbed in and were driven by the driver to Bromley House. They got out and were just going to go into the house when a telegram boy came up and told Fuster that a telegram was waiting for him in the house. We quickened our pace to the house and the door was opened to our knock and we put our hats and coats on the hall-stand and Fuster picked up and opened the telegram which said:-

> Mother seriously ill. No hope of recovery.
> Come at once. Brooks.

Fuster collapsed on a chair and put his face in his hands and sobbed. At last he said, 'Nayland Smith, this is the biggest blow I've ever had. My mother is dead, so I take it from this telegram.' Suddenly the light was lit and we found ourselves covered by two revolvers. 'Ha, Ha, Mr Fuster, so you see what your little plan has come to. Mr Smith, this is one of the most famous bank note forgers ever known. He was luring you to this house and almost succeeded. Well we've got – good heavens man! look there.' Nayland Smith followed the finger of Inspector Briggs for so the man with the revolver was. From the ceiling was dripping water, was it water? no it was blood. 'By gad' ejaculated Smith, and with one bound he cleared five stairs and made his way to the room above, closely followed by the Inspector. He opened the door and saw a ghastly sight. A young woman was lying on the floor with her head all bashed in by a steel club that was now in the hand of an ape, which was cowering in the corner. Blood was flowing freely from the wound in the girl's head. She was as dead as a doornail. Nayland Smith produced a revolver and shot the ape. Suddenly there was a muffled shot from downstairs and a groan. We looked at each other and went downstairs and saw Fuster lying, dead from suicide with a pistol, on the floor. The summed up case that Nayland Smith told the court the next day was as follows, – 'I was lured to Bromley House by a faked up story, which seemed to come more true by a telegram telling of the supposed dead Mother. Fuster was going to murder me with a mad ape in a steel room but instead of me being killed, his wife who had been feeding the ape had been seized by it and killed. Fuster is, or rather was, a famous bank note forger, and but for the timely arrival of Inspector Briggs I would have been dead at the present moment. Here ends the case ladies & gentlemen.'

William Sansom wrote to me in 1958: 'Should you by chance like the story with Nayland Smith as hero – some belated apology must be due to Mr Sax Rohmer.'

Angus Wilson 1913–

Kensingtonian

aged 16

Everyone must surely at some period in his life have endured the torture of staying in a private hotel or a boarding-house; the writer of this article has endured more than his fair share of this penance; he feels that he would like to give others some idea of its intensity in order that they may at least sympathize.

The Theosophists have a theory that your lot on earth is judged by whether you tried to do more than you could in the previous existence. The denizens of Kensington and Bloomsbury must have surely been ambitious beyond imagination; for theirs (I refer to the hotel populations) is not a happy fate; they none of them like their life; indeed their two consolations are that their fellow inmates like it less, and that they are only there temporarily. It seems as if I were mixing them up with mental deficients, but this is not the case. It is quite usual to hear a Kensingtonian of at least twenty years standing telling friends, 'Of course, my dear, we're only here for a time, the food isn't very good, and I don't care for the people, but you can do as you like, no restrictions, you know. It might be one's home.' It is quite awful to imagine the ideas that Kensingtonia possesses of 'one's own home'; in fact any private hotel, of which one can say nothing else in praise, appears to be in the gravest danger of becoming 'one's own home'.

The larger proportion of Kensingtonians, young and old, belong to that vague class which calls itself 'the new poor', or sometimes more internationally, '*les nouveaux pauvres*'.

It is the duty of these people: 1) To remember better days. 2) To say the country is going to the dogs. 3) Always to have known what it would be if you educated the other class.

All taxes, whether they are placed on imported glass or farm implements, cut down the income of the *nouveaux pauvres*, – 'Of course, at one time my husband and I . . . but since the war, you know, and what with taxes . . .' Such a conversation may be heard a dozen times a day. The new poor have friends in all the Government offices and most of the foreign Cabinets, who tell them State secrets in a most carefree manner. It is the work of '*les nouveaux pauvres*' to pass these on to Kensingtonia in general in a very secretive, hidden manner. Should one fail, however, to grasp the import of the hints which they make concerning matters which 'I'm afraid I can't tell you, it's not you, my dear, of course, but if you tell it to one person it may spread anywhere,' then they become most annoyed and often tell you outright in their anger.

They are largely 'retired' and play bridge, but there are a great number of younger 'new poor', who try vainly to keep up an air of modernity and naughtiness. They have naughty stories at their disposal by the hundred, and speak of actresses by their Christian names. Their experience[s] with the great, though largely imaginary, are nevertheless vastly entertaining. It is these young dashers who keep the coffee stalls going. They rush round to the station and get sandwiches at twelve o'clock at night; they find it 'so amusing'. If you wish to hear Mayfair's adjectives of two years ago, visit Kensington's bright young things. It is their custom also to visit night clubs; though at least one lady I know walks twice round South Kensington Station, has a cup of coffee at the ABC, slips secretly back to her room, and the next morning – 'Such an amusing evening, my dear, we danced till three, and Archie got very tight. Too bogus.' And so it is.

Then there are the 'weirds', poor, dotty old things, who drift from hotel to hotel. They're really more of a tragedy.

And, lastly, there are a few highbrows, whose main enjoyment is 'making fun of people'. They constantly wish that they could write. 'It would make such an amusing book.' Some of them do write short stories about Kensingtonia, and try to get them accepted for magazines, which is exactly what I am trying to do . . .

Dylan Thomas 1914–1953

Clown in the Moon

aged 14

My tears are like the quiet drift
Of petals from some magic rose;
And all my grief flows from the rift
Of unremembered skies and snows.

I think, that if we touched the earth,
    It would crumble;
It is so sad and beautiful,
So tremulously like a dream.

Of any Flower

aged 15

   Hourly I sigh
For all things are leaf-like
   And cloud-like.

   Flowerly I die,
For all things are grief-like
   And shroud-like.

The musical setting that Daniel Jones composed for the poem by his friend and contemporary Dylan Thomas at Swansea Grammar School on 20 April 1929. The poem is entitled 'Of any Flower'.

David Gascoyne 1916–

On the Terrace

aged 16

A heavy day; so old the sky
That covers up the tree-grown leagues below;
So slow the figures up and down
The terrace where the dusty fountains blow.

Here comes a colonel; at his side
His wife, with drooping shoulders, dressed in black.
They neither of them speak a word.
The colonel walks with hands behind his back.

The woman wears a fading rose
Upon her breast. She and the colonel stare,
Dumb at the footworn paving-stones
As they walk on. A sigh disturbs the air.

Stirred by no dull regrets for youth
Or love now dead that once in Spring was new,
Too tired to speak of memories,
They pause and turn to contemplate the view.

Then they pass on. A fountain leans
To drench the stones on which they stood with spray;
And from an iron-railinged tree
A bird looks after them – then flies away.

Homage à Mallarmé

aged 16

Returning from pure space, undazzled, to
this calm square room where, sitting quite alone,
I am within white walls; attaining through
lack of motion the quietness of stone;

(too absolute is cold, this hanging air
is null; outside the window no clouds pass;
immobile is this table and this chair;
here dreams a single rose within a glass);

returning to my room from emptiness,
my slowly-moving eyes rest on a page
where clear-cut words are printed, motionless,

and through these crystal words, sans youth, sans age,
to space I now return, expressionless,
from which my sight had made its pilgrimage.

From *Opening Day*

aged 16

CHAPTER 2

. . . 'Next week you are going to school,' said Mrs. Hutton. 'You are sure to be quite happy there, because I have been myself to speak to the matron about you, and besides, the Close is so lovely.'

All the way down to the meadow Leon told himself: 'Next week I am going to school. Next week I am going to school. Next week –' He did not dare to investigate in his mind what this entailed but simply uttered the fact to himself over and over again. 'Next week I am going to school,' he told the meadow. 'Next week I am going to school,' he told the stream. He said the same thing to the cows and to the wych-elms. But none of them took the slightest notice of him.

During that last week his Olympia[1] became somewhat dilapidated. He became unable to observe the state of the sky because of a newly-discovered obsession for the future. A drab yellow tinted the wholesome assistants of everyday.

Somehow he arrived. With Mrs. Hutton, a tall shadow, at his elbow, he emerged from the High Street Gate on which King Edward stood staring stupidly, not looking at all regal, perched on a pedestal, and realized that there was the tallest spire in England, swooping out of the foliage of the limes and that all the buildings he could see were very old and important and that they all belonged to very old and important people.

The front of the school, confronting a large rectangular space of gravel and beyond that confronting a larger rectangular space of grass, somewhat worn in patches, out of which rose two newly painted white goal posts, all ready to devour muddy spheres of leather on mild October afternoons, was quite deserted. No one was to be seen. But Mrs. Hutton unfastened the creaking gate of the headmaster's house, which latter had been stuck on to the main school building and looked somewhat out of place. A low brick wall separated the head master's front garden from the rectangular space of gravel and along it stood a row of hollyhocks and a row of geraniums. The front door was

[1]Typewriter.

painted white and above the slight porch was a plaster replica of an owl, also white. Mrs. Hutton groped among the jasmin that crawled about on the porch, for the bell, and, having found it, pulled it.

A slovenly maid appeared after some minutes, scowling at them through the half-opened door. 'What name?' she demanded.

'It's Master Brinson,' said Mrs. Hutton, as though she did not wish it to be thought that she was his mother.

'Come this way please,' and the maid showed them into a sitting-room. There were several figures on the mantelpiece and several shields on the walls, Leon managed to observe before Mr. Stratford entered. He was smiling. A tall, average-looking man in black, with a clergyman's collar. He shook hands with Mrs. Hutton and put his hands on Leon's shoulders. 'So this is Leon. Well, my boy, I'm sure I –'

'I must go now, dear. Be a good boy, won't you, and be sure to write every week,' and she lowered her sterile cheek for him to kiss. When she had gone Mr. Stratford took Leon out into a cold stone passage, full of a strange conglomeration of smells, and opening a door ushered him into the dining-hall. There was silence. Fifty faces stared at them.

'This is Brinson, a new boy. Look after him properly. He'd better sit next to you, Cody.'

When Mr. Stratford had gone, talking, or rather shouting, was resumed. The boys that were nearest to him asked him questions and Leon managed to murmur vague replies. He was in desperation as to what to do. He could not sit there for ever, motionless, answering questions like an oracle. He snatched a piece of bread and butter from the plate nearest to him, and having crammed it into his mouth, washed it down with a gulp of cold, watery tea.

'The greedy little pig,' someone said, 'did you see that?'

Leon turned pink and then red and then scarlet. His ears tingled. His eyes smarted.

Someone said: 'You may go,' and everyone crowded out of the door. Leon followed them. He found himself standing in the passage with his back to the wall. The floor seemed to be made of tombstones. There were a lot of coats hanging up and peculiar perfumes rolled to and fro. A tall boy came up to him and said:

'What's your name?'

'Brinson –'

'How old are you?'

'Eight and a half.'

The boy moved away, saying 'Brinson' to himself down the corridor.

There was a large schoolroom panelled with aged oak, its black surface covered with dates and initials and the portraits of deans, benefactors and the old boys who were killed in the War. In this room, dark in spite of five tremendous windows, clocks and desks and stoves and cupboards and pianos and blackboards remained in a state of permanent petrifaction. Boys and masters, matrons, servants, clergy-men and visitors came into the room and behaved in various ways and were all gone out again at least before half-past ten, but the blackboards, pianos, cupboards, stoves, desks and clocks took none but a slight and passive notice of them and always retained exactly the same form and almost exactly the same position.

Leon sat at the back of this room in a desk that contained a peculiar and individual smell that was, though he was not then able to analyse it, composed mainly of mouldy horse-chestnuts and cheap ink. Sitting in this desk with a copy of Somebody-or-other's *French Beginners* before him, open at a page which showed a picture of a pseudo-Gallic village complete with mountains in the distance, the lower strata of which were green with firs and the upper blue with ice and snow, he could see by looking carefully past the plaster bust of Handel that stood in the small window above the door that led out, by five stone steps, into the gravel court-yard, the cross on the top of the Cathedral, skilfully moulding itself from the rarified sunset air, and he thought of the two legends concerning the ball on which it stood, one of which declared that it contained the robes of the Blessed Virgin brought back reverently by Crusaders, and the other stated that it was so large that a coach and four could turn round upon it. The second story, he decided, could not possibly be true.

During his first term Leon did not belong to the Cathedral choir. He went to the Cathedral twice every Sunday with those others who also were not choristers.

The Cathedral astonished one as one approached it. From lawns of an exemplary smoothness stretched out square and flat almost all the way round it, it shot up suddenly towards the clouds, (there were almost always clouds; the spire seemed to magnetize them), rugged Gothic cliffs of an astounding vigour. Out of the grass it rose like a tremendous tree, petrified and sterilized in all its diversity of ornamental foliage by some antique winter of prodigious violence. This winter could always be felt inside the Cathedral as the builders had imprisoned its very soul in the gargantuan stone pillars, eternally grey. Even in the midst of summer the brilliant sunshine that rolled through the coloured windows seemed to be reflected from snow. And in this gothic forest of stone-foliaged pillars played at endless goblin pranks the gargoyles and those mythical monsters their tame companions. The spirits of the dead passed in a slow, invisible procession for ever up the nave. Inside the Cathedral time was condensed into merely the meaningless murmur of the bells imprisoned in the spire.

In the second term Leon became a member of the choir. Every service was to him a wonder. At Evensong, when a subdued and vernal twilight penetrated the very ancient windows, bathing the tombs in beauty, they sang long and dramatic operatic anthems by Stainer and Sullivan, or passages taken from the *Elijah* or the *Messiah*, with lengthy passages of recitative for the bass and impassioned choruses about the Daughters of Zion and the Redeemed of the Lord and They that sow in Tears. The organ made the stone floor, richly inlaid with mosaic, to rumble and the violet stretch of air between the high, carved, choir-stalls to quiver. At last the Archdeacon reached the word 'evermore' and the choir said 'Amen' and waited in silence for a moment until the organ began to fill the still, chill stretches of emptiness with deep, purple notes, warm, like velvet, like chastened orchids, when the choir, wine-coloured and white, rose from their places and wound slowly out through the gilded, heavily-detailed gates to their quiet vestries.

Each day of the week became a carefully erected structure, of which the main framework was always the same but the ornamentation was of seven different varieties. So many things to think about at once that it became difficult to retain one's balance. There were moments full of pleasure. Others were irksome. Out of the confusion arose the Cathedral that dominated every one's life there.

And there were new dreams to be woven. He had leisure – and perhaps an hour awake upon a hard pillow, when the ceiling at which he stared became transformed into a phantasmagoria that slowly slided from a waking into a sleeping dream. A region mystic and refined, a theory perverse but idealistic. A living phantasy, indeed, that was at one moment morose and at another capricious. Imagining himself alternately a superman and a pariah. The ghosts of characters from books followed him about and murmured in his ear at the wrong moment and led him to afterwards regretted actions. Walking of a grey morning through the Close he would become unaware of the arrangement of the paving-stones at his feet and would be in reality (that was more real than tangibility) transversing the regions of Doré illustrations to *Don Quixote*.

All this, of course, was annoying to his teachers. And each moment grew and swelled and joined the next moment until quite a large lapse of time had formed.

The limes cast shadows thicker than darkness over the green in front of the school, swimming in warm air. Through the open door that opened on to the courtyard, under the small window on the sill of which stood a plaster bust of Handel, flowed a smoke-stained cascade of light, yellow, brilliant. Outside in the warm night, beyond the reach of the courtyard, voices were uniting and creeping quietly over all the objects near. The notes of the part-song climbed up in a string through the faintly clattering lime leaves and upon reaching the empty stretches of air above the top of the trees, descended and followed one another in a close chase over the warm grass. People in coats stood grouped together listening underneath the limes. The concert was over. That was why there were clouds of tobacco smoke floating in the yellow light of the almost empty schoolroom. Leon stood with his hands in his pockets, alone, in the thick lime-tree shadows. The subdued notes of the last part-song mingled with tobacco smoke and a dog's bark and whispered conversations and the creak of a gate (that swung white for a moment in the gloom) and mounted slowly in a tepid stream of sound through the trees, through the broad expanses of the air of this summer night towards the spire. Somebody swung a hand-lamp. Somebody came crunching along the road that led through the Close. Somebody said: 'We had better go in now.' That was the end of the Summer Term.

The broad stretches of ploughed field that followed one another almost to the sky-line were as brown as a wholemeal loaf. The distant figures of the ploughman and his gaunt horses seemed to belong to a painting by Millet. A group of boys in blue caps and black suits with white linen frills round their necks passed chattering along the path that skirted the edge of the autumn fields. Leon was talking to the master who was in charge of the walk about Dickens. On one side of them were golden trees, and on the other, the fields, the brown, ploughed fields. There was no grass. On the other side of Leon walked Hugh Ashburne. Hugh Ashburne said that he couldn't read Thackeray. Mr. Dukes, taking his pipe out of his mouth, asked had they read Hugh Walpole because *Fortitude* was really a very fine book. Presently they came to a hedge with a stile in it which they all climbed. In front of them chalk-scarred hills sloped down into the valley out of which the spire stood pointing up through the mist. The brown ploughed fields stretched away behind them almost as far as the sky-line.

Leon swam in grey, shallow waters, among indefinite and half-formed thoughts, half-awake and more than half-asleep. He had almost forgotten the arrangement of the walls of the dormitory. There was a dressing-gown at the foot of the bed which had long blue-and-white tassels which dangled over the floor and somebody had bought it at Selfridge's, either on Monday or Tuesday, and somewhere there was some bath-water running away and someone was snoring and the wind was blowing quite hard outside and his bed was very warm and
. . .

Suddenly there was a noise. The window had blown open and the curtains were waving and flapping in the room. Somebody stood silhouetted against the panes. It was Hugh Ashburne. He was shutting the window. His bed was next to Leon's, and he came back across the dormitory, his bare feet padding on the linoleum. His hand brushed lightly across the quilt and he whispered 'Leon.' Leon was wide-awake but he did not reply. Hugh Ashburne got back into bed. Leon could see his white face staring across the carpet. Leon put out his hand and touched the floor. He felt the edge of the carpet. It was rough. It was made of coco-nut matting. He felt the linoleum. It was cold. He felt a warm, firm hand fingering his own. Hugh Ashburne pulled Leon towards him. Leon lay half across the chair that stood between their two beds. The warm, firm hand was brushing his hair back from his forehead. Nobody spoke. Everyone else was asleep. Hugh had a beautiful face. It was close against his own. The only sound was the thumping of their two hearts. After a time Leon crept back to his own bed. Hugh Ashburne's face stared across the carpet. Somewhere inside him he felt a strange new pain that he had never known before. He fell asleep.

Time passes. The stairs of the morning are erected every twenty-four hours across the sky and are folded up and packed away again every evening. Organ recitals do not as a rule interfere with exams but they are apt, to some people, to appear more important, more real. Nothing exists, to some, but the world of their own creation. If exams do not appear in the world of this creation they do not exist. One cannot pass things that do not exist. Time passes and brings along on its invisible back, at regular intervals, different kinds of exams. There are in these exams subjects which do not exist in the world of one's individual creation. Mathematics are meaningless. Latin is a methodical gibberish. Leon did not pass any exam, much though his father desired him to do so. Mr. Brinson said Leon was lazy. In reality Leon was not lazy because exams did not exist.

It is not difficult to say good-bye to people for whom you have no deep affection. Hugh Ashburne had left before him, so Leon said good-bye not so much to people as to a state of life deeply rooted by long acquaintance. The Close, when he left it, was green with Spring rains. Lilac was beginning to form in the gardens. The spire rose like a stately virgin into the pale sky. The whole valley was still but for a tinkling of streams in the hollows of the hills. The train which was carrying Leon away to London sent long, wavering plumes of smoke over the fields, starred with buttercups, that bordered the Cathedral city.

Mr. Brinson's business now kept him permanently in the City. No longer did he set out on long journeys into the provinces. He joined the bowler-hatted army of the 8.29 express. Accordingly he sold the Fordingbridge bungalow, forgot about his wife, and acquired a highly respectable mansion half-way between Richmond and Twickenham. Leon was lazy, he could not pass his exams so it was here that he had to idle away his time, waiting till he should be old enough to wear a bowler hat and join the solemn daily pilgrimage to the City.

It was here that he now knelt in front of the gas-fire on a raw Friday morning with the thin rain toppling stupidly among the chimney-stacks outside. Mrs. Hutton entered the room to clear the table. She said:

'Get up, stop dreaming, and go and write a letter to your grandmother.'

He had been among his memories for less than half an hour.

. . . Although the work of Van Gogh [Leon thought] exists on a plane much nearer to reality than that of Rimbaud, they have a very faint connection, for, while Rimbaud's world is an intensely unreal one, he conveys to the reader by his method of description, by his style, a semblance of truth; and the world of Van Gogh, while being intensely real, is conveyed to the spectator by a technique so unusual and so unique, that chairs and boots, shops and sunflowers take upon themselves an aspect that hitherto we had not suspected, an aspect that makes these wholesome, everyday objects seem strange and unreal, endowed with forces that we rather doubt belong to them, just as we decidedly doubt the possibility of the artificial world of Rimbaud. Thus the work of Van Gogh is the very inverse of that of Rimbaud, for while each important facet of the two geniuses are related, they are related in such a way that one is the very reverse and the negation of the other.

Penelope Fitzgerald 1916–

The Kitchen Drawer Poem

aged 15

The nutcracker, the skewer, the knife,
are doomed to share this drawer for life.

You cannot pierce, the skewer says,
or cause the pain of in one place.

You cannot grind, you do not know,
says nutcracker, the pain of slow.

You don't know what it is to slice,
To both of them the knife replies,

with pain so fine it is not pain
to part what cannot join again.

The skewer, nutcracker and knife
are well adapted to their life.

They calculate efficiency
by what the others cannot be,

and power by the pain they cause
and that is life in kitchen drawers.

Keith Douglas 1920–1944

Chapter of Autobiography

aged 12

As a child he was a militarist, and like many of his warlike elders, built up heroic opinions upon little information, some scrappy war stories of his father. Most of the time he was down in the field, busy, with an absurdly puposeful look on his round face, about a tent made of an old sheet, and signposted with a board saying 'sergeants' mess'. He was quite at home there for hours, while he was four and five, telling himself stories as he ran about, and sometimes stopping a moment to contemplate the calf who shared that field, a normally quiet animal, but given to jumping five-barred gates. As you would expect, he played with lead soldiers, and toy artillery, and was most fond of the cavalry and the highlanders. Unlike the other troops who either marched sedately with sloped arms or sat bolt upright on their caracoling steeds, the highlanders were charging, their kilts flying at a swift angle out behind them and the plumes upon their heads also flying out, though often in the wrong direction for the broken heads were fixed back on with matches, and swivelled easily.

His father did not spend very much time with him, but would speak to him of war and boxing and shew the boy his great muscles, for here at least he could shew them off to unbounded admiration. He teased his son, and pinched and tormented him sometimes, but Keir liked his father better than his mother, who fondled him a deal too much and cried sometimes, even then Keir and Billy Cameron who lived near, were often about together in trees. They built a house once, in the big tree at the end of Billy's garden, but Billy fell out of it. So they were kept away from there and played in the garden itself. Captain Cameron entertained them with a service revolver and a bomb, but in the end they were left to themselves.

'My father,' said Billy, 'shot a German point blank. He saw him coming out of a pillbox and shot him before the German could shoot

Daddy.' Keir was a little annoyed that Billy should tell this story, condensed though it had become, so often. But point blank was admittedly a good thing to say and in return he explained how his own father was shot by a Turk.

'*My* father wouldn't have let a measly old Turk shoot him,' said Billy and Keir's reposte was squashed. Yet he was very proud of his father and went home to his supper sadly down the road past Miss Drivers, and Colonel Transome, the old man who was so funny because he never wore a waistcoat, and Miss Peck and Mr Peck who made cider, and each of the other neighbours whom Keir pictured not by remembering their faces, but the colour of their front hedges and fences. He reached up and opened his own front door, which had a high knob. His father was inside, taking off his shoes, in a good temper. 'Hallo, Old Bean,' he said 'been climbing trees?' Keir beamed. He loved to be called Old Bean. 'Hallo dadda, Captain Cameron threw a bomb at me.' 'Oh, you didn't mind though did you? You're a tough guy.' 'Gee whiz I'm a tough guy, Daddy, tell me about Yukon Jake again.' Captain McDonald raised a chair in one hand and shook it. He recited ferociously.

Yukon Jake
was as tough as a stake,
hardboiled as a picnic egg.
He combed his hair
with the leg of a chair
and drank his beer by the keg.

Keir repeated it furiously and with great pleasure. 'Now teach me to box' he said. He was not restrained from punching his father's amateur-champion broken nose by the entry of his grandfather, Mr Castellain, a courteous and courtly old gentleman who now spent his life playing patience. Mr C. received the bomb story less enthusiastically. He had once been in the volunteers, but had never fought anyone in his life. Harrow and Balliol and an addiction to natural history and good manners had made him a quiet spoken and kindly old man. Considerate and unselfish to his own class but almost unaware of the existence of any other.

The smell of his supper, which was a kind of broth prepared by his grandmother attracted Keir into the other room. 'Where's Mummy?' he asked Mrs Castellain. 'She went down to the village, dear, to do some shopping. Now go and wash your hands before you eat your supper. There's a good boy.' Probably that type of phrase annoys every child. It galled Keir, anyway, and he said pettishly 'Don't want to wash my hands. They're quite clean. I want my supper.' 'Now don't be rude to Granny. Go and wash.' 'I won't wash my hands –' Keir was beginning when his father came in and told him angrily to hurry up and go, and Keir went.

When he was coming downstairs he heard his mother come in through the front door. She looked pretty but tired out, and smiled at Keir who was a consolation to her for many things. 'I'm going to eat my supper Mummy.' 'All right dear, I'll come and watch you.'

Keir ate his supper, and talked a good deal, in spite of the reprimands of his grandmother, who still thought that little boys should be seen and not heard, and often said so. Outside the evening sunlight reminded Keir of fairies, for it did indeed endue the garden with a dreamlike quality. So he demanded a story from his grandfather, who was in the drawing room playing with cards.

'Very well, little man, I'll tell you a story in one minute, when I've finished this game of patience,' said his grandfather, in his curious calm voice which held no trace of foreign accent though its polite unruffled tones themselves must have come over the channel with his own grandfather, escaping the revolution by the aid of servants to whom he, luckily, had been kind.

Keir waited two minutes before he asked for his story again, and received the same answer, out of the corner of his grandfather's mouth, as the card game, for long the most exciting part of the old gentleman's life, drew to its most exciting moment and completion. The minutes continued to drag slowly by, and at last, Keir realised that he would soon be hauled storyless to bed. When he had asked once more and received the same unhurrying answer, he suddenly grew furious, and overturned the old gentleman's precious ricketty table.

Mr Castellain had never been so near anger in twenty years. But after Keir's simple explanation that he wanted his story, he said kindly, 'You're sorry you turned my table over, aren't you, little man?' And on Keir's admission of penitence (for he saw that would begin his story soonest) the story was begun.

In the morning Keir was woken by the sun and the birds and lay in bed listening to them and thinking to himself, until it occurred to him that people were about in the house and his mother's and father's beds were empty. He went and peered out, and saw through the bannisters a group of people standing in the hall, about his mother, who lay asleep on a stretcher or as it seemed to Keir a funny sort of bed. He realised almost at once that his mother was ill and ran downstairs on his bare feet asking what was the matter with her, as they took her away out of the front door. Someone he had never seen took him back to his bed with some unsatisfying explanation, and locked the door on him. He began immediately to scream and beat upon it, but they had all gone and he was alone, locked in. He became frantic, fell on the floor and shouted curses he had heard 'Curse damn bother darn bloody' in a string as long as he could put together, until he got up from the floor and hit his head on the door knob. It hurt and with some idea of punishing the door knob he hit his head on it five or six times more, very hard, and then subsided on the bed sobbing.

In a few minutes his grandfather came up and succeeded in calming him, explaining that his mother had an illness, called Sleepy Sickness, but she would be well soon, when she had gone to the Hospital and had a rest. With that, for the moment, Keir was content.

Mummers

aged 14

Put by your stitching. Spread the table
With winking cups and wines. That sable
Doff for your brighter silks: are all
Your glints of pearly laughter shuttered?
See where the outdoor snows, wind-fluttered,
Through the arched window fall.

See where the deep night's blast has straddled
The ancient gargoyle, weather-addled
And striped with melted tapestry
Of snow; his evil face well carven
By Brother Ambrose, lean and starven,
Celt-fasting, rich in artistry.

Soon come the masked mummers, knocking
With hard snow-rod. The door's unlocking
Answers the stars with indoor light.
Now to the drum-tap, with snow crusted
Cardboard steed, and ancient rusted
Blade, the Saint and Turk will fight.

Strange Gardener

aged 16

Over the meadows,
framed in the quiet osiers, dreams the pond,
region of summer gnat-busyness,
where, in the afternoon's blue drowsiness,
fish plop among the water-shadows:
and the cool trees wait beyond.

A young man dwelt there,
with a swift, sad face, and full of phantasy,
repeating, as he heard it,
the alliterative speech of the water-spirit;
smoothing his pale hair
with automatic ecstasy.

This was his garden,
uncultivated, (order hated him)
whence, in a winter-madness,
(whose scourge filled him with recklessness,
seeing the frost harden),
the water-spirit translated him.

EXPLANATION

A   Scheme
(i) I have not kept very strictly to any metre, but the metre is, roughly:

$$- u\, u - -$$
$$u - u - u - u -$$
$$u - u - u - u$$
$$- - - u\, u - u\, u$$
$$u - u - u - u$$

[last line missing in original school exercise book]

(ii) The scheme of rhyming is:

A
B
C
C   Last syllable only rhyming
A
B

B Meaning

Over the meadows . . .
cf Frederick Prokosh

The first line is intended to take the reader well away from his surroundings immediately.

framed . . .

you are a rook flying over the pond, and looking down at it.

the quiet osiers. . .
cf. F. P.

you know they are there, like a flame, but their rustling is inaudible, you are not distracted from the important thing, the pond.

gnat-busyness. . .

this is not, of course, a spelling mistake, but quite a different word from business.

fish plop among the water-shadows

you have flown over the meadows as a bird.

Now you are a water-being, hanging over the pond in the summer.

trees *wait* beyond. . .

these did not distract you from your contemplation of the pond, but they are there for you, when you are ready, to look at them.

a swift, sad face. . .
the main idea of this verse is taken from the chief character of 'The Star-born'

the swiftness of his face is in the lines of it, his high cheek-bones and the curved hang of his hair. It is his eyes that are sad, because his thoughts are more beautiful than reality.

repeating . . . the alliterative speech. . .
this idea also from 'The S-b'

he repeats it, struck with its beauty, as a child will repeat what is said to it.

alliterative. . .

the speech of water is an interminable cavalcade of similar sounds.

automatic ecstasy. . .
his pale hair . . . C. Day Lewis in 'From Feathers to Iron' speaks of 'two-headed poets'

he is not aware of his action, but the feel of his hair, soft and smooth under his hand gives him pleasure. Cf. T. S. Eliot 'she smooths her hair with automatic hand'.

a winter madness . . .
seeing the frost harden. . .
this has some connections with 'The Tempest' Doth suffer a sea-change' cf. translated'

The sight of the beauty of summer dying all about him caused him such acute misery that he was temporarily mad.

the water-spirit translated him. . .

i.e. he drowned himself in the throes of his despondent insanity. For the water-spirit cf. Henry Williamson 'The Star-born'.

General

This explanation is intended to show that although the main idea of the poem was spontaneous, and the poem itself is short, the scheme behind it is lengthily and carefully thought out. The lapses in metre are put in purposely, in an attempt to make it less stereotyped and more interesting.

A lino-cut made by Keith Douglas to go with his poem 'Strange Gardener', first published in 1936 by Christ's Hospital School magazine called The Outlook.

Philip Larkin 1922–1985

We see the Spring breaking across Rough Stone

aged 15

We see the spring breaking across rough stone
    And pause to regard the sky;
But we are pledged to work alone,
    To serve, bow, nor ask if or why.

Summer shimmers over the fishpond.
    We heed it but do not stop
At the may-flies' cloud of mist,
    But penetrate to skeleton beyond.

Autumn is the slow movement;
    We gather our harvest and thank the lofty dusk.
Although glad for the grain, we are
    Aware of the husk.

And winter closes on us like a shroud.
    Whether through windows we shall see spring again
Or not, we are sure to hear the rain
    Chanting its ancient litany, half-aloud.

Having grown up in Shade of Church and State

aged 16

Having grown up in shade of Church and State
    Breathing the air of drawing-rooms and scent,
Following the Test Match, tea unsweet in Lent,
    Been given quite a good bat when aged eight,
With black suit, School House tie, and collar white,
    Two hair-brushes and comb, a curl to coax,
He smiles demurely at his uncle's jokes,
    And reads the *Modern Boy* in bed at night.

And when, upon the cricket-field, he bats,
    – All perfect strokes – (one sees the dotted line)
And with a careful twelve tries not to vex,
    We hear the voice: 'Y'know, he's good! Why, that's
A graceful player!' True? Perhaps. Benign,
    We diagnose a case of good old sex.

Francis King 1923–

Other Town

aged 15

There have been other loves, and other afternoons,
When, in the certain frenzy of a new creation,
Above the symphony, we heard the mocking voice
And knew that there could be no other choice.

There have been other days, when other words were spoken:
The laughter froze upon the death-mask of the hero,
And so the grieving summer or the late November
Gave us a moment that we could remember.

There have been other worlds, and other words of wisdom,
But only for the dead or for the never-living:
For those who did not love, or loved and lied
The order of the fast is petrified.

There have been other ways, and other hopes were spoken
By those who were supremely young or greatly happy:
But 'I' is always 'I', and still the constant lover
Endures the knot of self he cannot sever.

To a Friend

aged 15

With some remembrance of a sure, unsought caress,
　　The wisdom of the past, the wish for peace and pardon,
　　A word beneath the willows in the lovers' garden,
We shall regret the summer's ravished tenderness.

You, who were kind, and I, who felt the need for pity,
　　Returned, disconsolate, to woo the common day:
　　There were no candles lit to guide us on our way
Above the argument and order of the city.

We two – the young, the sad, the foolish – did not find
　　Death's compromise an easy bargain for our fears;
　　Still through the vacant panorama of the years
We feel the solitude, the fever of the mind.

These things must fade: the happiness that could not last,
　　The sound of laughter, and the long retreat from pain,
　　The brush of lips, the touch of fingers in the rain,
And all the rest and respite of the living past.

Yet, at this hour, because I know that you are near,
　　Your eyes to find some comfort in a sad pretence,
　　Your hands to stress a moment's brief impermanence,
I shall not be afraid to meet the things I fear.

Alison Lurie 1926–

Poem

aged 15

I would be up and out
Where the cold wind blows
On the westward road
Where the river flows.

I shall walk by the field
Or through if I choose
And scuff the brown grass
Under my shoes.

I shall go all alone
With the wind in my face,
I shall walk swift and far,
I shall set my own pace.

Elizabeth Jennings 1926–

A Dead Bird

aged 13

I held it in my hand
With its little, hanging head,
It was soft and warm and whole
But it was dead.

Anthony Thwaite 1930–

Chirico Landscape

aged 16

The walls ascend the sky in squares of light,
The shadows slant, the murals of the air
Gleam in the bright intrinsic wealth of sun.
Statues are posed beside an endless sea,
Where waves fall geometric, copper-curved,
In vast extremes of shadowless blue planes.
Houses fall inward, black dust filters through
The planetary rain. Silence runs cracks
Through fever whitened earth. The sun pours down
The opaque cloudless skies; the moon limps through
The purple heavens with a ring of light.
And through the brittle air the stranger hears
The dull, resounding echo from his tomb.

Sylvia Plath 1932–1963

I Thought that I could not be Hurt

aged 14

I thought that I could not be hurt;
I thought that I must surely be
impervious to suffering –
immune to mental pain
or agony.

My world was warm with April sun
my thoughts were spangled green and gold;
my soul filled up with joy, yet felt
the sharp, sweet pain that only joy can hold
can hold.

My spirit soared above the gulls
that, swooping breathlessly so high
o'erhead, now seem to brush their whir-
ring wings against the blue roof of
the sky

(How frail the human heart must be –
a throbbing pulse, a trembling thing –
a fragile, shining instrument
of crystal, which can either weep,
or sing.)

Then, suddenly my world turned gray,
and darkness wiped aside my joy.
A dull and aching void was left
where careless hand had reached out to
destroy

my silver web of happiness.
These hands then stopped in wonderment,
for, loving me, they wept to see
the tattered ruins of my firma-
ment.

(How frail the human heart must be –
a mirrored pool of thought. So deep
and tremulous an instrument
of glass that it can either sing,
or weep.)

You Ask me Why I Spend my Life Writing?

aged 15

You ask me why I spend my life writing?
Do I find entertainment?
Is it worthwhile?
Above all, does it pay?
If not, then, is there a reason? . . .

I write only because
There is a voice within me
That will not be still.

The first poem was inspired by the accidental smudging of a pastel still-life which
Sylvia Plath had just completed. Her mother, grandmother and brother were
admiring it, when the doorbell rang. Going to answer it, her grandmother took off
her apron and it brushed against the drawing, smudging part of it.

Beryl Bainbridge 1934–

From *Filthy Lucre*

aged 13

Gasper Liverwick slouched down the back streets. He made his way through the many alleys, and finally reached Thames Street. Here the lamps were yellower, the public houses more frequent and the people more degraded.

If, dear readers, when you come to the words 'public houses' and see in your mind's eye the bleary eyes and wasted limbs of the men and women staggering from such places, their yellow-skulled babies mewling in the gutters, do not call a curse on the wretched mortals who so displease your thoughts! Rather, call a fervent curse on the nobles and bishops of our London, for not giving the poor support and, what is more, self-respect – for regarding the silken coats of their many horses with delight, and for ignoring the parchment skins of their fellow-humans breeding and dying and neither eating or living, from one end of the town to another. When a heart is sick, and a mind stunted without education or enlightenment, when bodies curve unhealthily and carry disease in a warped line from head to toe, it is surprising how a glass of ale or spirits fills the guts and brain-matter with explosive feelings of relief, temporary well-being and a kind of gaiety. That is why the poor drink. To them the public houses, with warm fires kept burning to tempt the passer-by, serve as vast communal homes. Little matter that even their small coins go once more to furnish the rich brewery-owners with finer clothes and bedding, with more silken horses to pull their ladies' carriages, with more power to extract rents, taxes and tolls . . .

Drawing by Beryl Bainbridge, aged 13

Thomas Keneally 1935–

Those Nazarene Days you could see a Child

aged 16

Those Nazarene days you could see a Child
Sitting on the stones near the dirt green patch
Where the winds of ages had etched and slowly wiled,
From their purse, the bronze-burnished denarii of the desert.
Here the children played when the grass was rich.
How it heckled round their blustering feet
When the fishers with their fish fought
With housewives near the soiled, tangent street.
They would be prog-browed, looking at the pantomime
Of pincered faces. And this Child all the time,
Lost in the holocaust of thrifty words,
Seemed in a heaven untouched by human minds.
One day the fishers I have spoken of
Were spitting out the sins of the old city,
And telling of a certain Clausos: 'Pity!
Clausos was caught this week for dodging dues:
They daubed the poor Jew on a Roman cross
And sieved him with a multi-crimsoned lance.'
That night we see – the intermittent pants
Of light on the pall and languorous parchment lawn;
And we hear that queer child weep all night till dawn.

Keneally writes: 'Age: sixteen. Inclination: Australian-Irish holycard mysticism.'

Piers Paul Read 1941–

White Stone, Crystal Stone

aged 13

White stone, crystal stone,
   You've seen the ages pass,
From then till now, you've seen them through
   Those slender blades of grass.

White stone, crystal stone,
   You've seen all things go by,
You've seen the path that time did take,
   From the place where now you lie.

White stone, crystal stone,
   I leave you in the sun
That shines on and always will,
   For all the time to come.

Ted Hughes 1930–

Wild West

aged 15

I'll tell you a tale of Carson McReared,
Who, south of the 49th was feared
Greater than any man ever before,
And men went in fear of his .44,
For he'd shoot the ears from any man
From Two-gun Ted to Desperate Dan.
His hoss's name was Diamond Ace
And he'd spit the teeth from a rattler's face,
He was 12 years old when he first ran wild
Because a teacher got him riled.
The sheriff and posse rode him into the hills,
'Cos he shot away the teacher's frills.
So he pulled his guns (his father's gift)
And as the sheriff drew, he gave him a lift
Over the edge of a cliff quite high,
With a .44 slug in either thigh.
Then he turned his guns on the sheriff's men
And shot 'em dead. Yeah, all the ten.
Then he saddled his hoss and rode away
To the land where Kinkaid the Marshall held sway.
'Twas in the street that the two first met,
And the sight of the bad man made Kinkaid sweat,
Then like a flash the two men went,
And Carson McReared the Terrible sent
A leaden slug weighing 200 grains
Slap into Kinkaid's squirming brains.
Then turning to his hoss he strode,
Leaving Kinkaid the Marshal dead in the road;
And all the town gaped with shock and fear,

Lest they should feel the burning sear
Of a rifle slug around their liver –
A thought which made the brave men shiver.
This check the President could not stand,
So he ordered the law with an iron hand
To encircle Carson with an armoured ring
And make him on a Redwood swing.
So 15 marshals and umpteen men
Hied them forth to Carson's den,
Carson McReared the terrible killer,
The man with a hide like an armadillo.
'Twas in Grand Canyon where they came to grips,
And with steely eyes and firm set lips
1,200 men on spirited hosses
Charged him regardless of all losses,
So Carson stood with his back to the wall,
Triggered his guns, and shot 'em all.
But alas! he too was shot to hell,
No more would he drink in the 'Southern Belle';
And knee deep in blood, where he had to paddle
Stood Diamond Ace, with an empty saddle.

Envoi

Paris, October 10, 1958

Mr. Neville Bra~~y~~brook
10 Gardnor Road
London N.W.3
England

Dear Mr. ~~Bragbrook~~,

I hope I have got your name right, but it was
not easy to make out.

You would be surprised how many dozens of anthologies exactly like yours have been planned, and
then abandoned. Nobody wants his earliest and
worst writing to be perpetuated. Such a collection
would be nothing but a big bore. Saroyan once
thought of getting out an anthology of everybody's
worst piece, and then realized how awful that would
be.

Sincerely yours,

James Thurber

Sources

The Editor and Publishers have made every effort to trace the copyright holders of each item in this book. They would be pleased to hear from any who have not been acknowledged and will put this right in future editions. A word of explanation, too, about the publication dates given below. Often as long as a year could pass between the time that an item was composed and its subsequent publication in a school magazine.

CONRAD AIKEN: 'Number 58' and 'Lex Talionis' from *The Anvil*, the magazine of Middlesex School, Concord, Massachusetts, U.S.A. Copyright © 1904. Reprinted by permission of Brandt & Brandt Inc.

W. H. AUDEN: 'The Traction Engine' and 'The Engine Room.' See Note in text. Copyright © 1937 by the Estate of W. H. Auden. Reprinted by permission of his literary executor Edward Mendelson.

BERYL BAINBRIDGE: Extract from Chapter 4 of *Filthy Lucre* (1986) and drawing from Chapter 9. See Introduction. Copyright © 1986. Reprinted by permission of the Author and Gerald Duckworth & Co Ltd.

W. N. P. BARBELLION: 'The Naturalist,' 'Squirrels' and 'Wild Duck' from *The Journal of a Disappointed Man* (1919). W. N. P. Barbellion was the pseudonym of Bruce Frederick Cummings. The entries from his journal are dated 2 April 1903, 24 December 1903 and 7 December 1907.

JOHN BETJEMAN: 'The Snow,' 'Summer Poem' and 'Ode on a Mid-Victorian Ornament.' 'Summer Poem' appeared in *The Draconian*, the magazine of the Dragon School, Oxford, 1920. Reprinted by permission of the Estate of Sir John Betjeman and John Murray Ltd. The facsimile of 'Snow' is reproduced by permission of Christopher Peter, the Modern Librarian Archivist, at the University of Victoria, British Columbia, Canada.

JOCELYN BROOKE: 'Surrey' from *The Wind and the Rain Easter Book* (1962). Copyright © 1962. Reprinted by permission of the Estate of Jocelyn Brooke.

ROY CAMPBELL: 'Now like a Ghost in Shadow Lands' from his *Collected Works* (1985). See Note in text and *Roy Campbell: A Life* by Peter F. Alexander (1982). Reprinted by permission of his grandson Francisco Campbell Custodio and Ad. Donker (Pty) Ltd.

G. K. CHESTERTON: 'Worship' and 'Idolatry' from *The Journal of the Junior Debating*

Club, St Paul's School, 1891–92. See *The Tablet*, 18 May 1974.

CHRISTOPHER DAWSON: 'The Gold City and the Coal City'. Unpublished. Copyright © 1989. Reprinted by permission of his daughter Christina Scott.

KEITH DOUGLAS: 'Chapter of Autobiography' from *Keith Douglas: A Miscellany* edited by Desmond Graham (1985), and 'Mummers' and 'Strange Gardener' from *The Complete Poems of Keith Douglas* (1978). Copyright © Marie J. Douglas 1978 and 1985. Reprinted by permission of his literary executor J. C. Hall and the Oxford University Press. Lino-cut for 'Strange Gardner' from *The Outlook* (1936) reprinted by permission of his literary executor J. C. Hall.

T. S. ELIOT: 'A Lyric' and 'The Man who was King' from *The Smith Academy Record*, April and June 1905. See Introduction. 'A Lyric' reprinted by permission of Mrs Valerie Eliot, Faber & Faber Ltd and Farrar Straus & Giroux Inc. from *Poems Written in Early Youth* (1967) and the short story 'The Man who was King' reprinted by permission of Mrs Valerie Eliot and Faber & Faber Ltd from *The Smith Academy Record*, June 1905.

RONALD FIRBANK: *Lila* and 'The Wind & The Roses'. See *Ronald Firbank* by Miriam J. Benkovitz (1969) for history of the unfinished novel *Lila* and for details of the privately printed edition of 'The Wind & The Roses' by Alan Clodd in 1965. *Lila* reprinted by permission of A. P. Watt Ltd. on behalf of Colonel Thomas Firbank.

PENELOPE FITZGERALD: 'The Kitchen Drawer Poem.' Unpublished. Copyright © 1989. Reprinted by permission of the Author.

E. M. FORSTER: 'The Opinions of Mistress Whichelo' and 'The Influence of Climate and Physical Conditions upon National Character.' See Introduction and Note in text. 'The Influence of Climate and Physical Conditions upon National Character' comprise the concluding ten surviving paragraphs of a prize-winning essay written at Tonbridge School in 1897 and included in the school magazine. Both items reprinted by permission of King's College, Cambridge and the Society of Authors as the literary representative of the E. M. Forster Estate.

DAVID GASCOYNE: 'On the Terrace' and 'Homage à Mallarmé' from *The New English Weekly*, 27 July 1933 and *The Sunday Referee*, 24 September 1933. Copyright © 1933. Extracts from Chapters 2 and 3 of *Opening Day* (1933). Copyright © 1933. Reprinted by permission of the Author.

JOHN GRAY: 'Writ by Me when I was Sixteen Years Old.' See Note in text and *In the Dorian Mode: A Life of John Gray* by Brocard Sewell O. Carm. (1983).

ROBERT GRAVES: 'The Dying Knight and the Fauns', 'The Miser from Shenham Heath' and 'Merlin and the Child.' See Introduction. Reprinted by permission of A. P. Watt Ltd. on behalf of the Executors of the Estate of Robert Graves.

HENRY GREEN: 'Sermon'. See Note in text. Copyright © 1942. Reprinted from *Pack my Bag* (1942) by permission of Chatto & Windus Ltd.

GRAHAM GREENE: 'Confessions' from *The School Gazette*, Berkhamsted School, quoted by the author in *A Sort of Life* (1961). Copyright © 1961. Reprinted by permission of Laurence Pollinger Ltd and International Creative Management Inc.

A. E. HOUSMAN: 'Summer', and 'Letter Home' from *Alfred Edward Housman: Re-*

collections (a special issue of *The Bromsgrovian*), published by Bromsgrove School in 1936, and *The Letters of A. E. Housman*, edited by Henry Maas (1971). Reprinted by permission of the Society of Authors as the literary representative of the Estate of A. E. Housman.

RICHARD HUGHES: 'Explanation, on Coming Home Late'. See *This Way Delight*, edited by Herbert Read (1953). Reprinted by permission of David Higham Associates Ltd and the Estate of Richard Hughes.

TED HUGHES: 'Wild West' from *The Don and Dearne*, the magazine of Mexborough Grammar School. Copyright © 1946. Reprinted by permission of Olwyn Hughes.

CHRISTOPHER ISHERWOOD: 'Mapperly Plains', written when he was sixteen at Repton, but first published in the third volume of *Public School Verse*, edited by Martin Gilkes, Richard Hughes and P. H. B. Lyon (1923). He was listed on the contents page as C. W. B. Isherwood. See *Exhumations* (1966). Reprinted by permission of the Estate of Christopher Isherwood and Methuen Ltd.

ELIZABETH JENNINGS: 'A Dead Bird'. Unpublished. Copyright © 1989. Reprinted by permission of the Author and David Higham Associates Ltd.

DAVID JONES: Drawings of 'Lion' and 'Dancing Bear' from *The Wind and the Rain Easter Book* (1962). See Introduction and Note in text. Copyright © 1962. Reprinted by permission of the Trustees of David Jones.

JAMES JOYCE: 'O Fons Bandusiae'. See Book III of Horace's Odes (no XIII) and *James Joyce* by Richard Ellman (1959). Copyright © 1959. Reprinted by permission of the Society of Authors as the representative of the Estate of James Joyce.

THOMAS KENEALLY: 'Those Nazarene Days you could see a Child'. See Note in text. Unpublished. Copyright © 1989. Reprinted by permission of the Author.

FRANCIS KING: 'Other Town' and 'To a Friend' from *The Salopian*, the magazine of Shrewsbury School. Copyright © 1938. Reprinted by permission of the Author.

RUDYARD KIPLING: 'The Carolina', 'Overheard' and 'Roses' from *Early Verse by Rudyard Kipling 1879–1889*, edited by Andrew Rutherford (1986). See Introduction and Note in text. 'Overheard' and 'Roses' were included in *Schoolboy Lyrics* (1881). 'The Carolina' is taken from the holograph version in the Kipling Collection, Dalhousie University Library, Canada, signed J. R. Kipling. It is reprinted by permission of the Oxford University Press from *Early Verse by Rudyard Kipling 1879–1889*. © The National Trust for Places of Historic Interest or Natural Beauty, 1986.

PHILIP LARKIN: 'We see the Spring breaking across Rough Stone' and 'Having grown up in the Shade of Church and State' from the *Collected Poems* of Philip Larkin, edited with an introduction by Anthony Thwaite (1988). Copyright © 1988. Reprinted by permission of the literary executors of the Larkin Estate.

T. E. LAWRENCE: 'Playground Football' and 'Playground Cricket' from *The Oxford High School Magazine* (*O.H.S. Magazine*), 1904. 'Playground Football' was published under the pseudonym of 'Goalpost.'

WYNDHAM LEWIS: 'Good Times'. Unpublished. © P. Wyndham Lewis and Mrs G. A. Wyndham Lewis by kind permission of the Wyndham Lewis Memorial Trust (a registered charity). Acknowledgement is also made to Cornell University for kindly providing photocopies of the original manuscript and drawings.

MALCOLM LOWRY: 'Hockey Dramatics' and 'A Rainy Night' from *The Fortnightly*, the magazine of the Leys School, Cambridge. Copyright © 1926. Reprinted by permission of the Estate of Malcolm Lowry and Sterling Lord Literistic Inc.

ALISON LURIE: Poem. Unpublished. Copyright © 1989. Reprinted by permission of the Author.

KATHERINE MANSFIELD: 'The Sea', 'The Three Monarchs' and 'In the Tropics' transcribed by Margaret Scott from notebooks dated 1903. Unpublished. Copyright © 1989. Reprinted by permission of the Estate of Katherine Mansfield.

GEORGE ORWELL: 'Awake! Young Men of England' and 'Kitchener' from *The Henley and South Oxfordshire Standard*, 2 October 1914 and 21 July 1916. Copyright © 1914 and 1916. Reprinted by permission of the late Sonia Brownell Orwell and Secker & Warburg Ltd.

RUTH PITTER: 'Field Grasses' from *The New Age*, 11 May 1911. Copyright © 1911. Reprinted by permission of the Author.

SYLVIA PLATH: 'I Thought I could not be Hurt' and 'You Ask me why I spend my Life Writing' from *Letters Home: Correspondence 1950–1963*, edited by Aurelia Schober (1975). Copyright © Ted Hughes. Reprinted by permission of Olwyn Hughes.

WILLIAM PLOMER: 'Epigram: to a Profane but Entertaining Friend in a Tent' from *William Plomer: A Biography* by Peter F. Alexander (1989). Copyright © 1989. Reprinted by permission of Sir Rupert Hart-Davis.

BEATRIX POTTER: 'London' and 'Sunday March 12th 1882' from *The Journal of Beatrix Potter: 1881–1897*, transcribed from her code writings by Leslie Linder (1966). Copyright © Frederick Warne & Co., 1966. Flower drawing of foxglove and periwinkle. Copyright © Frederick Warne & Co., 1955.

EZRA POUND: 'Limerick' from *The Jenkinstown Times-Chronicle*, 7 November 1896. It was signed E. L. Pound. See Note in text. Copyright © 1972 by the Estate of Ezra Pound. Reprinted by permission of the Ezra Pound Literary Property Trust, Faber & Faber Ltd and New Directions Publishing Corporation.

ANTHONY POWELL: Drawing of 'Colonel Caesar Cannonbrains of the Black Hussars' from *The Eton Candle* (1922). Reprinted by permission of David Higham Associates Ltd.

JOHN COWPER POWYS: 'Corfe Castle' from *The Wind and the Rain Easter Book* (1962). See Introduction. Copyright © 1962. Reprinted by permission of the Estate of John Cowper Powys.

KATHLEEN RAINE: 'On an Autumn Evening'. Unpublished. Copyright © 1989. Reprinted by permission of the Author.

PIERS PAUL READ: 'White Stone, Crystal Stone' from *This Way Delight*, edited by Herbert Read (1953). Copyright © 1953. Reprinted by permission of the Author.

WILLIAM SANSOM: 'Caught in his Own Trap' from *The Wind and the Rain Easter Book*

(1962). See Note in text. Copyright © 1962. Reprinted by permission of the Estate of William Sansom.

SIEGFRIED SASSOON: 'Something about Myself' and 'In the Churchyard' from *Poet's Pilgrimage* by Dame Felicitas Corrigan OSB (1973). Copyright © 1973. Reprinted by permission of Stanbrook Abbey.

BERNARD SHAW: 'Strawberrinos: or, The Haunted Winebin'. See *The Collected Letters of Bernard Shaw: Vol I*, edited by Dan H. Laurence (1965–88). Reprinted by permission of the Society of Authors on behalf of the Bernard Shaw Estate. Drawing of St John the Baptist reprinted by permission of the Society of Authors on behalf of the Bernard Shaw Estate. Copyright © 1989.

STEVIE SMITH: 'Spanky-Wanky' from *Stevie* by Jack Barbera and William McBrien (1985). See Note in text. Reprinted by permission of James MacGibbon.

DYLAN THOMAS: 'Of any Flower' and 'Clown in the Moon' from *The Poems of Dylan Thomas*, edited and introduced by Daniel Jones (1971). Copyright © 1971. Reprinted by permission of David Higham Associates Ltd. Musical score 'Of any Flower' reprinted by permission of the composer, Daniel Jones, and David Higham Associates Ltd. Copyright © 1989.

EDWARD THOMAS: 'Dad' from the Edward Thomas Colbeck Collection in the University of British Columbia, Canada. It has not been published before in its entirety, although parts of it were included by George R. Thomas in *Edward Thomas: A Portrait* (1985). Copyright © 1989. Reprinted by permission of his daughter Myfanwy Thomas.

ANTHONY THWAITE: 'Chirico Landscape' from *Piazza*, a literary magazine of Kingswood School, Bath. Copyright © 1947. Reprinted by permission of the Author.

EDWARD UPWARD: 'Gloom' from *The Reptonian*, the magazine of Repton School. Copyright © 1919. Reprinted by permission of the Author.

SYLVIA TOWNSEND WARNER: 'Upon the Quality Called Romance' was included anonymously by her father George Townsend Warner in his book *On the Writing of English* (1915), but is now generally assumed to be by her. See *Sylvia Townsend Warner* by Claire Harman (1989). Copyright © 1989. Reprinted by permission of the literary executors Susanna Pinney and William Maxwell of the Estate of Sylvia Townsend Warner.

EVELYN WAUGH: 'The Curse of the Horse Race' and *'Multa Pecunia'*. See Introduction and Note in text. Unpublished. Copyright © 1989. Reprinted by permission of Peters Fraser & Dunlop Group Ltd. Acknowledgement is also made to the Harry Ransom Humanities Research Center, the University of Texas at Austin, for kindly providing photocopies of the original manuscripts and drawings.

BEATRICE WEBB: 'Castles in the Air' and 'Mormons' from *The Diary of Beatrice Webb: Vol. I, 1873–1892*, edited by Norman and Jeanne MacKenzie (1982). The Passfield Papers © The London School of Economics and Political Science, 1983. Reprinted by permission of Virago Press Ltd and Harvard University Press.

H.G. WELLS: 'The Desert Daisy' posthumously published from the original

List of First Lines

Acknowledgements

I should like to thank the following who have helped me in various ways in the compiling of this book: the late Conrad Aiken, Peter Alexander, Paul Bailey, Quentin Bell, Colin Benford, the late John Betjeman, the late Elizabeth Bishop, Gordon Bowker, the late Jocelyn Brooke, Robert Burchfield, Lucy Burgess of Cornell University, Susan Chitty, Alan Clodd, Dame Felicitas Corrigan OSB, Peter Dickinson, C. J. Fox, P. N. Furbank, Philip Gardner, Stephen Gill, Desmond Graham, the late Robert Graves, John Hall, M. A. Hall, the Modern Archivist at King's College, Cambridge, Claire Harman, Cathy Henderson of the University of Texas, Thomas Hinde, Michael Holroyd, Ralph Izzard, A. Norman Jeffares, the late David Jones, Daniel Jones, Dan H. Laurence, Norman MacKenzie, Robyn Marsack, Edward Mendelson, Michael Millgate, Peter Parker, Omar S. Pound, the late William Sansom, Margaret Scott, the Rev. Brocard Sewell, O. Carm., the late Stevie Smith, Linden Stafford, Jon Stallworthy, Julian Symons, Myfanwy Thomas, Anthony Thwaite, S. K. Tulloch the senior editor of New Words in the Oxford English Dictionary, the late Evelyn Waugh, Sir Angus Wilson and the late Rev. Andrew Young. As always, the staff of the British Museum Reading Room and the Department of Manuscripts have been a pleasure to work with. A general word of thanks is also due to many school librarians. Grace Ginnis typed often from faded originals – no one could have been more painstaking. Richard Cohen my publisher made many valuable suggestions. Last, but in every other sense first, there remains my wife whose enthusiasm for the project never waned and from whose advice I gained at every stage: no editor could have had a more encouraging collaborator.